The Forward book of Poetry

2020

This anthology was designed and produced by Bookmark, sponsor of the Prizes. Bookmark is a global content and communications company based in London, Toronto, Montreal, Santiago, Lima, New York, LA, Shanghai and Singapore. Bookmark uses consumer insights to develop compelling content for brands that engages consumers and drives sales. Clients include Patek Philippe, Air Canada, LATAM, Bombardier, Explora, Standard Life, American Express Travel, Christie's, Lindt, Silhouette, Hudson Yards, Pandora, the Academy of St Martin in the Fields and StreetSmart. bookmarkcontent.com @bookmarkcontent

The Forward Book of Poetry

2020

London

First published in Great Britain by
Bookmark · 83 Clerkenwell Road · London ECIR 5AR
in association with
Faber & Faber · Bloomsbury House · 74-77 Great Russell Street
London WCIB 3DA

ISBN 978 0 571 35388 0 (paperback)

Compilation copyright © Bookmark 2019
Foreword copyright © Shahidha Bari 2019
Cover image copyright © Jamie Keenan 2019

Printed and bound by CPI Group (UK) · Croydon CRO 4YY

A CIP catalogue reference for this book
is available at the British Library.

To Felicity Ann Sieghart with love and thanks

Contents

Highly Commended Poems 2019

Foreword

When the team behind the Forward Prizes invited me to chair this year's judging panel, my response was to agree immediately. 'I am a poetry person,' I said, as though that explained everything. But over the course of the year – from the intensive reading of the spring, to the delightful, sometimes pained, summer of judging – I have revisited that instinctive response and wondered what I meant by it.

Does the old distinction, between people who read poetry and those who don't, still hold up? As poetry publishers in the UK experience an unprecedented boom, with sales up 50 percent over five years and a record 1.3m books sold in 2018, it seems everyone is reading poetry. The Forward Prizes have always sought out work that matters to a general reading public as well as poetry devotees. The prizes are driven by the conviction that, deep inside, we are all poetry people.

How readily you can work out what a poem means does not matter. The pleasure comes from handling them, often clumsily, puzzling over them, worrying over them, misunderstanding them entirely, dismissing some of them wrongly, then revisiting them wiser. It comes from loving old poems devotedly and being startled by new ones. Being a poetry person means permitting yourself to be stopped in your tracks by a particular arrangement of language.

In the run up to the shortlisting for this year's prize, each judge submitted a personal longlist, with the final selection being drawn from those individual preferences. Curiously, despite our experience – the five-strong jury featured three poets – we were all plagued by anxiety. Placed next to the expert lists prepared by others, would ours point to our poor judgment? It was reassuring, then, to discover how unexpectedly those lists converged and how bracingly they differed. This anthology is a reflection both of that harmony and that diversity.

You'll find contributions from long-established poets we know to revere, beloved poets, dear to our heart, obscure poets' poets, and poets who were entirely new to all of us and no less staggering in their talents. One of the greatest privileges of judging is to be invested with the power to write new names into the roster of contemporary poetry. Whether they proceed to win or not, all the poets in this anthology warrant your attention. They are here because we celebrate them and invite you to do so too. There are young voices next to older voices, the work of men, women and non-binary identifying poets, writers from Britain and from far beyond it.

If poetry gets to the heart of things, judging should have given us a frontline view of the human condition in 2019. We can report back that your concerns include, as fellow judge Tara Bergin has succinctly observed: 'Horses, taxis, blood...'. Other themes emerged too: grief, meditations on motherhood, anguish over notions of nationhood, a rich vein of landscape poetry next to equally beautiful cityscapes.

Deep in our reading, it became clear how often our writers reached to poetic forms to capture individual experiences of trauma and collective experiences of tragedy. It is a reminder of how poetic forms serve us in articulating desperate things, and how in a moment of need, the line that comes to you is incalculably precious, offering sympathy and a sense of solidarity. Disillusionment, both personal and political, concerns about mortality, illness, aging – poetry gives voice to those experiences. But satire, puckish humour, sly puns – they, too, emerged with remorseless glee in the works we read.

The technical proficiency of contemporary poetry was evident to us. But it's harder to share with you how beautifully prepared so many of the collections were. Slender books meticulously dressed, elegant typefaces, illustrations, papers delightful to the touch. None of the judges would be foolish enough to judge a book by its cover, but it was moving nonetheless to gain a sense of the care with which collections are being assembled and how precious a book can be made to feel. If it was reassuring to see the continuing quality of the work commissioned by our leading poetry publishers, it was inspiring, too, to see the nobility of small presses putting forward new poets for us to treasure.

Above all, the submissions startled us with their boldness, their willingness to test the boundaries of what a poem could look like (Ann Wroe's biography-in-verse, *Francis*) and how it could be performed (Ilya Kaminsky's *Deaf Republic*). Many of you will know how exhilarating the spoken word scene has felt of late – exceptional performers feature here too (Inua Ellams, Jay Bernard). Some of the most distinctive submissions challenged us to imagine a poetry that could be still closer to theatre, compelling us to see how powerfully its compact form could stage the drama of our personal and political lives.

In classrooms all over, English teachers regularly instruct their pupils to 'read out loud' with the hope they might better understand the sound of verse. But this year's poetry crop also reminded us that we can read inwardly, that poems are not just heard but felt in the shape of the words formed in our mouths, understood resonantly deep within, too.

We are all poetry people. You read the right line at the right moment and suddenly the world is illuminated with a different light. If you are searching for that line, we have confidence that you will find it. And if you've ever doubted that poetry is for you, know that it takes just one poem to turn a reader into a lifelong poetry person – and then you'll never look back. There's every possibility that you'll find it in here.

Shahidha Bari
Chair of the judges
June 2019

Preface

Back in 1992, *The New Yorker* published a Martin Amis short story
contrasting the lives of two writers. The first, a scriptwriter, sends
his screenplay to *Little Magazine*, hoping that this time, maybe, it will
be accepted for publication. The other, Luke, faxes a sonnet to his
agent and heads for the gym. Within hours Hollywood producers are
vying to fly him to LA for development meetings. He takes his travel
arrangements for granted. 'In poetry,' Amis wrote, 'first class was
something you didn't need to think about. It wasn't discussed. It was
statutory. First class was just business as usual.'

Amis's witty reversal of the starving poet stereotype still has shock
value. Yet although poets in general still earn pitifully little, the story
wouldn't work so well today: in 2019 a poet creating a blockbuster
no longer seems absurd.

Poets are commandeering the stages of the National Theatre,
headlining major festivals, taking major prizes (British Podcast Awards,
Rathbones Folio). The sales of poetry books are rising and their readers
are young: two-thirds aged 34 or under.

A 2018 survey of school-age students shows that almost half choose
to engage with poetry in their free time, often on screens. They
watch, create and share short films in which language is used artfully,
rhythmically, in which words and silence are deployed with skill, whether
performed by one person or several. The gap between screenwriting
and poetry is shrinking.

At least two of this year's contenders for the Forward Prizes – poetry
collections by Ilya Kaminsky and David Cain – could, without a stretch,
be staged in their entirety as compelling dramas, while also rewarding
the reader who lingers on every line. Kaminsky's *Deaf Republic* has
already been broadcast on BBC Radio 4, voiced by actors Fiona Shaw
and Christopher Eccleston.

Other books have been honed by years of reading and performance
– works by Raymond Antrobus and Jay Bernard are in the running for
the Best First Collection award but a quick glance at YouTube confirms
their authors are no novices. If you've been to Tate, Glastonbury,
Latitude, the Edinburgh Festival, or just listened to local radio, your
ears will have encountered many of the poets featured here.

Where does this leave the Forward Prizes for Poetry, founded in the year of that Amis story, when books ruled supreme and poets had to wait for years for a publishing house to bring out their work? Forward Arts Foundation is proud to champion poetry in all its shapes through National Poetry Day, but these particular prizes still celebrate the written form – words that lay claim to a permanence that outlives pixels on a screen, that need no batteries, chargers, sockets.

In turning the pages of this book, which includes work by more than 65 poets, all published between September 2018 and September 2019, I have tapped into a source of renewable power. No poet here creates for public performance alone: each dreams of their words receiving the slow consideration and repeated reflection that only an individual can give.

The final selection grew from many hours of quiet contemplation and lively discussion from our judges, who spent months with the 204 volumes of poetry and 183 individual poems we sent them. Thanks, then, to writer and broadcaster Shahidha Bari, poets Tara Bergin, Andrew McMillan and Carol Rumens, and the British Library's Jamie Andrews for their attentiveness and generosity in tackling mountains of poetry books.

Thanks are also due to Casey Jones, Chris Carus, Fay Gristwood, Alex Courtley, Lucy Coles and Simon Hobbs and everyone at our sponsors, Bookmark – the content marketing agency formerly known as Forward Worldwide. Bookmark has supported us from the very start: its dedication over the past 28 years is an example to all in literary sponsorship. As well as supporting the prizes, its staff invest a huge amount of expertise and time in the creation of this book.

We are grateful to Arts Council England, to the estate of the late Felix Dennis – which supports the Felix Dennis Prize for Best First Collection – and to the Esmée Fairbairn Foundation and the John Ellerman Foundation. Thank you, too, to fellow trustees of the Forward Arts Foundation, Martin Thomas, Robyn Marsack, Cynthia Miller, Giles Spackman, Bidisha and Kim Evans, and to outgoing trustees Joanna Mackle, Nigel Bennett and Jacob Sam-La Rose.

Thanks to the Foundation's staff: Susannah Herbert, the executive director, who continues to ensure these prizes punch above their weight and to Natalie Charles for her design eye and her focus on detail. Emily Hasler, John Clegg and Rachel Piercey have been intimately involved in the making of the book, ensuring the poets and their poems are represented properly. The team at SP Agency, Philippa Perry and Tatti de Jersey, have been terrific in promoting the prizes – and the anthology – this year, along with Hannah Jefferies of Communitas. The cover is the work of Jamie Keenan, recommended by Andrea Reece of National Poetry Day.

Finally, my thanks to Georgia Attlesey, Forward Prizes Manager, for bringing her undauntable good spirits and enthusiasm to so many aspects of this year's administration process.

William Sieghart
Founder of the Forward Prizes for Poetry
June 2019

Shortlisted Poems
The Forward Prize for Best Collection

Fiona Benson

[personal: speedo]

Before the beach
we stop
for a drink.
Zeus strips off
to a minuscule
red speedo
and bulges profanely.
I lapse my guard
and laugh
as he reclines
in the splay-legged
plastic chair.
It's a mistake.
He bolts upright.
I stir the ice
in my drink
and hold my breath
and listen
for the electricity
crackling across his skin
to rest.
Then I thank him
for the orange juice.
It's freshly pressed, I say,
the best I've ever tasted.
Zeus leans back once more
in his perilous chair
and watches
as the lovely nymphs
walk by
in neon bikinis,
the blades of their backs
shifting as they gesture

to each other.
I long to escape
in that conspiracy
of women.

Eurofighter Typhoon

My daughters are playing outside with plastic hoops;
the elder is trying to hula, over and over –
it falls off her hips, but she keeps trying,
and the younger is watching and giggling,
and they're happy in the bright afternoon.
I'm indoors at the hob with the door open
so I can see them, because the elder might trip,
and the younger is still a baby and liable to eat dirt,
when out of clear skies a jet comes in low
over the village. At the first muted roar
the elder runs in squealing then stops in the kitchen,
her eyes adjusting to the dimness, looking foolish
and unsure. I drop the spoon and bag of peas
and leave her frightened and tittering, wiping my hands
on my jeans, trying to walk and not run,
because I don't want to scare the baby
who's still sat on the patio alone, looking for her sister,
bewildered, trying to figure why she's gone –
all this in the odd, dead pause of the lag –
then sound catches up with the plane
and now its grey belly's right over our house
with a metallic, grinding scream
like the sky's being chainsawed open
and the baby's face drops to a square of pure fear,
she tips forward and flattens her body on the ground
and presses her face into the concrete slab.
I scoop her up and she presses in shuddering,
screaming her strange, *halt* pain cry
and it's all right now I tell her again and again,
but it's never all right now – Christ have mercy –
my daughter in my arms can't steady me –
always some woman is running to catch up her children,
we dig them out of the rubble in parts like plaster dolls –
Mary Mother of God have mercy, mercy on us all.

Niall Campbell

Clapping Game

(where [*] represents a clap of the hands)

The blue [*] night was on the [*][*] hill
and my [*] mind was working strangely
after a [*][*] day of [*][*] games

and then [*] and then [*][*], pouring out
some [*] red wine, and watching [*][*] as
the [*][*] moon took its high position,

above the [*][*] house, seeming like a [*]
stamp of something like [*][*] happiness,
I reached the point where the clapping stopped

and quiet in the house, night in the garden,
I was free to play that different game;
up late with the world, my small life leapt,
I rolled its dice across the writing desk.

The Night Watch

It's 1 a.m. and someone's knocking
at sleep's old, battered door – and who
could it be but this boy I love,
calling for me to come out, into
the buckthorn field of being awake –

and so I go, finding him there
no longer talking – but now crying
and crying, wanting to be held;
but *shhh*, what did you want to show
that couldn't wait until the morning?

Was it the moon – because I see it:
the first good bead on a one-bead string;
was it the quiet – because I owned it,
once – but found I wanted more.

Ilya Kaminsky

We Lived Happily during the War

And when they bombed other people's houses, we

protested
but not enough, we opposed them but not

enough. I was
in my bed, around my bed America

was falling: invisible house by invisible house by invisible house—

I took a chair outside and watched the sun.

In the sixth month
of a disastrous reign in the house of money

in the street of money in the city of money in the country of money,
our great country of money, we (forgive us)

lived happily during the war.

Deafness, an Insurgency, Begins

Our country woke up next morning and refused to hear soldiers.

In the name of Petya, we refuse.

At six a.m., when soldiers compliment girls in the alleyway, the girls slide by, pointing to their ears. At eight, the bakery door is shut in soldier Ivanoff's face, though he's their best customer. At ten, Momma Galya chalks NO ONE HEARS YOU on the gates of the soldiers' barracks.

By eleven a.m., arrests begin.

Our hearing doesn't weaken, but something silent in us strengthens.

After curfew, families of the arrested hang homemade puppets out of their windows. The streets empty but for the squeaks of strings and the *tap tap*, against the buildings, of wooden fists and feet.

In the ears of the town, snow falls.

Town

Vidyan Ravinthiran

Today

I was reading my book by the window
waiting for you when I noticed one flower
of those you'd artfully splayed had snapped.
Like a limp wrist the orange gerbera hung, and over
my knuckle it vented a beige gunge. As I snipped
the stem for a smaller vase, the glow
of the radiant petals was too much. Time lapped
me round, the day went unseized.
For this was no opportunity I could have missed;
only the lonely moment which blazed
in my hand, unplucked. Like many,
I had forgotten that time isn't money
and I don't need always to be on the move
within the world you've shown me how to love.

Aubade

It's Saturday but you haven't slept in.
Your side of the bed's still warm.
My hangover is like a smashed windscreen.
I hear a repeated noise down the corridor.
One surface determinedly rubs another.
While asleep I picked my lip till it bled
– a side effect of the medication,
like the gravid if sledgehammer-obvious nightmare.
Your body walks in completely naked.
This is how you prefer to clean the bathroom
and though my plan was for inertia
I understand today we're to redeem the time.
The sound of the curtains yanked apart
is the morning clearing its throat.

Helen Tookey

City of Departures

When I stepped out of the house the air held rain, the scent of it, the taste. The light was bruised and yellowish. A blackbird was singing, very clearly, his song amplified by the coming rain. The scene felt familiar, already lived-through. The caption was *Morning in the city of departures*. I was walking through narrow streets close to the docks, under the piers of bridges, through brick archways. The cobblestones were wet and I had on no shoes. There had been a railway accident, journeys were disrupted or rendered impossible. You didn't appear and yet you were present, if only in the feeling of missed connections. You were there in the sense of having spoken a vital word to me and then gone away, leaving me wandering the wet quaysides holding the word I couldn't use, a bright coin in the wrong currency.

Letter to Anna

Dear Anna, I shall come to you in November, all being well. They are making plans to close the borders, but I believe there is a little time yet.

Dear Anna, I am thinking of you in your city of water. Do you remember, when we walked out along the rampart, we saw so many herons, sitting silent in the trees like huge grey sentinels, we were almost scared, though we laughed about it afterwards.

Dear Anna, it is still summer here, but so heavy, it drags on one, it weighs one down. Yesterday I walked to the field to pick blackberries (they are early this year), and I got a good bowlful, but even such a short walk made me so tired. I think it must be fresher where you are.

Dear Anna, I look often at your picture, though I could wish he had not made it quite so sad – that look in your eyes, so far away, and that tilt of your head, as though you are listening for something, but you do not really believe it will come. There is something in the hands, too – somehow I think he has made them too large, almost like a man's hands, they seem to lie in your lap so awkwardly, as though you had yet to grow into them, yet to discover what they could be for.

Dear Anna, I have applied for my papers and shall come to you in November. I do not know whether there will be another opportunity. Please expect me.

Shortlisted Poems
The Felix Dennis Prize
for Best First Collection

Raymond Antrobus

The Perseverance

Love is the man overstanding
                Peter Tosh

I wait outside THE PERSEVERANCE.
Just popping in here a minute.
I'd heard him say it many times before
like all kids with a drinking father,
watch him disappear
into smoke and laughter.

There is no such thing as too much laughter,
my father says, drinking in THE PERSEVERANCE
until everything disappears —
I'm outside counting minutes,
waiting for the man, my *father*
to finish his shot and take me home before

it gets dark. We've been here before,
no such thing as too much laughter
unless you're my mother without my father,
working weekends while THE PERSEVERANCE
spits him out for a minute.
He gives me 50p to make me disappear.

50p in my hand, I disappear
like a coin in a parking meter before
the time runs out. How many minutes
will I lose listening to the laughter
spilling from THE PERSEVERANCE
while strangers ask, *where is your father?*

I stare at the doors and say, *my father
is working.* Strangers who don't disappear

but hug me for my perseverance.
Dad said *this will be the last time* before,
while the TV spilled canned laughter,
us, on the sofa in his council flat, knowing any minute

the yams will boil, any minute,
I will eat again with my father,
who cooks and serves laughter
good as any Jamaican who disappeared
from the Island I tasted before
overstanding our heat and perseverance.

I still hear *popping in for a minute*, see him disappear.
We lose our fathers before we know it.
I am still outside THE PERSEVERANCE, listening for the laughter.

Happy Birthday Moon

Dad reads aloud. I follow his finger across the page.
Sometimes his finger moves past words, tracing white space.
He makes the Moon say something new every night
to his deaf son who slurs his speech.

Sometimes his finger moves past words, tracing white space.
Tonight he gives the Moon my name, but I can't say it,
his deaf son who slurs his speech.
Dad taps the page, says, *try again.*

Tonight he gives the Moon my name, but I can't say it.
I say *Rain-nan Akabok.* He laughs.
Dad taps the page, says, *try again,*
but I like making him laugh. I say my mistake again.

I say *Rain-nan Akabok.* He laughs,
says, *Raymond you're something else.*
I like making him laugh. I say my mistake again.
Rain-nan Akabok. What else will help us?

He says, *Raymond you're something else.*
I'd like to be the Moon, the bear, even the rain.
Rain-nan Akabok, what else will help us
hear each other, really hear each other?

I'd like to be the Moon, the bear, even the rain.
Dad makes the Moon say something new every night
and we hear each other, really hear each other.
As Dad reads aloud, I follow his finger across the page.

Jay Bernard

Pace

I have seen the light you've seen
and my body has been where yours has been
some part of me resides where you reside
we've swapped presences and parting –

I have seen what you have seen
become the part of you I stood beside
passing friend with green eyes
I now reside where you reside –

hello, you standing there to the left of me
you in the heart of those hearing me read
further ahead on the road we are walking
there in the shadow performing in front of me –

you in the rhythm that's always unfolding
you are a question that's always been asked
who are we now and what are we wanting
from the voices you heard, the presences there –

how do we ask the quiet you've left
what voice you recalled
whose hand you were holding?

Sentence

If mum is in the living room / sister in the bathroom / then sentence
says / morning / the two have not yet / said their first words –

If mum is in the bedroom / sister in the bedroom /
then it is evening / and sentence says / sister is leaning against the
door, cross-legged / drawing –

If the two are in the kitchen / best friend also /
unzipping fish spine from / its studded silver flesh / then sentence says –

the wound around the waist of the house punctured / full of indoor
exits that do not close behind you / stairs / take you back to the start
/ what you were running from / dark warps the frame –

the people have taken their hands away from their eyes / and have
stapled their mothers and sisters to the underpass wall / their cousins
and brothers and lovers to the underpass wall / only the missing –
never the dead – to the underpass wall.

Not rivers, towers of blood.

David Cain

4.06pm

He was brought to me.

He was on a broken down billboard

Supported by two other football fans.

'Is there anything you can do for this boy?'

He was laid there and this police officer looked at me and he
went, 'Oh, he's had it.'

I remember looking down and I thought,

'Oh, my God, it's a little boy.'

The first thing I did was to try and feel a pulse in his wrist.

The pulse that I found was very, very feeble, but it was still there.

It was still there.

We made our way up the slope and into the gymnasium.

We were just told, if they were dead, injured or badly injured, to
take them there.

The two police officers who were with me said I'd actually done
too much.

I was to stay there with body 51.

I thought it would be best to give some sort of resuscitation.
I got down on my hands and knees and proceeded to give
mouth-to-mouth resuscitation.

I thought heart massage may have helped, and I did the worst
thing ever.

I actually picked him up which you're not supposed to, because
he could have had a neck injury of any sort.

I tried a second time, that's to say I picked him up.

I actually cradled him and I thought,

'You're not going to die. You can't die.'

I remember holding him and I thought, no, he's only a baby.

It can't be happening.

I had his head in my arms and so much of his back,

And that's when his eyes opened and he said, 'Mum'.

He looked straight through me.

Then his eyes closed and he just went very, very limp altogether,

So I placed him down on the ground and tried to give him
mouth-to-mouth again and heart massage.

That's when I felt a tap on my shoulder and it was another police
officer

And he said, 'Leave him. He's gone. There's nothing you can do.'

4.15pm

A gentleman began to shout into the back garden.

It wasn't in the days when we had mobile phones.

He asked us if we could telephone his mum and let her know that he was okay.

He was very pale, very upset.

I said, 'Of course you can, of course you can.'

After that, there was a succession of people with phone numbers, which we rang.

Isabel Galleymore

The Starfish

creeps like expired meat –
fizzy-skinned, pentamerously-legged,
her underfur of sucking feet
shivers upon an immobile mussel
whose navy mackintosh is zipped
against the anchor of this fat paw,
this seemingly soft nutcracker who exerts
such pressure until the mussel's jaw
drops a single millimetre. Into this cleft
she'll press the shopping bag of her stomach
and turn the mollusc into broth,
haul in the goods and stumble off,
leaving a vacant cubicle,
a prayer come apart.

Significant Other

A cloud takes on the shape of a tortoise.

The tortoise can never
repay the gesture. Unashamedly,

its owner once believed that it answered

hello in its reptilian hiss
as she once believed that he, who delighted

her body, delighted her body

only. Did the creature ever think
a thought her way?

The tortoise snaps its tortoisey jaws

eating all that's laid on
without looking up.

Stephen Sexton

Cheese Bridge Area

Why does it have to be like that?
   Why does what have to be like that?
Cracker Barrel. It's a weird shape.
   Well I don't mind. Does it matter?
No other cheeses are that shape.
   Some other cheeses are that shape.
It's not that really. It's just square.
   Well it doesn't taste square. It's cheese.
Maybe it's the square/cracker thing.
   Well not every cracker is square.
The crackers in the cupboard are.
   There are other kinds of crackers.
Maybe it's the Barrel part then.
   Well what's the problem with barrels?
I dream of someone throwing them.
   Do you know someone who does that?
It seems like a long time ago.
   It has nothing to do with cheese?
No the cheese just reminded me.
   Cheese can mean almost anything.

Front Door

In through the translucent panels of the front door stained with
    roses
here and there their green stems wander sun patterns the
    cavernous hall
with rose outlines the wood paneled box came sharp-cornered
    the TV
so heavy to look at it cut into my clavicle was it
full of cannonballs and was it carried on four or six or eight
sets of shoulders into the room such impossible heaviness
for the size of it and was it full of tinctures puzzled colours
picture elements their sweep rates flashing across it when I saw
my reflection in the blackness of its face it was a child's face.
Neighbours came over their fences a summer day but dark with
    storms:
a deluge impassible roads the forest lurching on the hill.
I felt my head turn into stone no it wasn't the old TV
we carried her to the window the meteors that time of year
Perseids only sparks really the Irish Sea fell from the sky
in bullets through the afternoon and Kong Kappa no King Koopa
navigates his ship through the storm an engine or thunder rumbles.
Electrons pooled under the clouds the room was heavy with ions.
I held my breath in the lightning the sea fell into the garden.
Evening rose like the river then the flash with all of us in it
and her voice moves around the edge of the world and now I
    think I
remember what I mean to say which is only to say that once
when all the world and love was young I saw it beautiful glowing
once in the corner of the room once I was sitting in its light.

Shortlisted Poems
The Forward Prize for Best Single Poem

Liz Berry

Highbury Park

In the woods at night men are fucking
amongst the gorgeous piñatas of the rhododendrons,
the avenue of cool limes.
By day I walk my son down the secret pathways,
smell the salt rime of sex on the wind,
a condom glowing with blossomy cum,
knotted and flung; I bury it gently
under the moss with my boots.
I envy them, these lovers, dark pines
beneath their knees, the tarry earth
opaline with the desire paths of snails,
fallen feathers in the dirt like warnings.
I know those days of aching to be touched
by no-one who knows you.
After he was born I wanted nothing but the wind
to hold me, the soft-mouthed breeze
coaxing my skin like the grass
from a trampled field.
How heavenly it seemed then, light shafting
emerald through wounded leaves,
the woods a church, we its worshippers,
and all that sex – freed from love and duty –
like being taken by the wind, swept
from the cloistered rooms of your life,
stripped and blown,
then jilted dazzling in the arms of the trees.

Mary Jean Chan

The Window

after Marie Howe

Once in a lifetime, you will gesture
at an open window, tell the one who
detests the queerness in you that dead
daughters do not disappoint, free your
sore knees from inching towards a kind
of reprieve, declare yourself genderless
as hawk or sparrow: an encumbered body
let loose from its cage. You will refuse
your mother's rage, her spit, her tongue
heavy like the heaviest of stones. Her
anger is like the sun, which is like love,
which is the easiest thing, even on the
hardest of days. You will linger, knowing
that this standing before an open window
is what the living do: that they sometimes
reconsider at the slightest touch of grace.

Jonathan Edwards

Bridge

Me? I get up early, see. I like
the hour or so before the cars arrive,
the city sleeping there over my shoulder,
the early morning sky that is all mine,
a few gulls spelling *Mmmm* out with their bodies.
I make the most of that because, by nine,

I bear the city's weight here on my back,
all these commuting cars and belching vans.
I hold my nose and try to keep control
with traffic lights: they lean out of their windows
to swear, to drop their rubbish, spit on me,
to smoke a cigarette and flick a burning

bit on me. The days I like the best
are Sundays, when I just lie in all day.
The acupuncture of a gentle moped,
or this hand-holding couple, afternoon,
who linger at my apex, make my view
the background to their love. I've heard it said

our card is marked, our day is done, what with
advances in technology, hot air
balloon and tunnels, gravity, but this
is human, really, to look at the distance
from here to there and say, well, what's the shortest
that could be? I do not like the nights:

the river's tinnitus, and the low hum
a taxi engine makes is like a dream
of my own snoring. Worst are those who come
to visit at that hour. Here, tonight,

a young man walks alone towards my middle,
dumb-belling a Scotch bottle underarm:

he reaches midway, looks down at the river,
then clambers over, stands there on the ledge
and holds on tight. I feel his warm touch there.
Oh souls, believe me, I'd never let go
if I could choose. I know by heart, exactly
what it is to just have too much weight to bear.

Parwana Fayyaz

Forty Names

I

Zib was young.
Her youth was all she cared for.
These mountains were her cots
The wind her wings, and those pebbles were her friends.
Their clay hut, a hut for all the eight women,
And her father, a shepherd.

He knew every cave and all possible ponds.
He took her to herd with him,
As the youngest daughter
Zib marched with her father.
She learnt the ways to the caves and the ponds.

Young women gathered there for water, the young
Girls with the bright dresses, their green
Eyes were the muses.

Behind those mountains
She dug a deep hole,
Storing a pile of pebbles.

II

The daffodils
Never grew here before,
But what is this yellow sea up high on the hills?

A line of some blue wildflowers.
In a lane toward the pile of tumbleweeds
All the houses for the cicadas,

All your neighbors.
And the eagle roars in the distance,
Have you met them yet?

The sky above through the opaque skin of
Your dust carries whims from the mountains,
It brings me a story.
The story of forty young bodies.

III

A knock,
Father opened the door,
There stood the fathers,
The mothers' faces startled.
All the daughters standing behind them
In the pit of dark night,
Their yellow and turquoise colors
Lining the sky.

'Zibon, my daughter,
Take them to the cave.'
She was handed a lantern.
She took the way,
Behind her a herd of colors flowing.
The night was slow,
The sound of their footsteps a solo music of a mystic.

Names:
Sediqa, Hakima, Roqia,
Firoza, Lilia, and Soghra.
Shah Bakhat, Shah Dokht, Zamaroot,
Nazanin, Gul Badan, Fatima, and Fariba.
Sharifa, Marifa, Zinab, Fakhria, Shahparak, MahGol,
Latifa, Shukria, Khadija, Taj Begum, Kubra, Yaqoot,
Fatima, Zahra, Yaqoot, Khadija, Taj, Gol, Mahrokh, Nigina,

Maryam, Zarin, Zara, Zari, Zamin,
Zarina,

At last Zibon.

IV

No news. Neither drums nor flutes of
Shepherds reached them, they
Remained in the cave. Were
People gone?

Once in every night, an exhausting
Tear dropped – heard from someone's mouth,
A whim. A total silence again

Zib calmed them. Each daughter
Crawled under her veil,
Slowly the last throbs from the mill house

Also died.
No throbbing. No pond. No nights.
Silence became an exhausting noise.

V

Zib led the daughters to the mountains.

The view of the thrashing horses, the brown uniforms
All puzzled them. Imagined
The men snatching their skirts, they feared.

We will all meet in paradise,
With our honored faces
Angels will greet us.

A wave of colors dived behind the mountains,
Freedom was sought in their veils, their colors
Flew with wind. Their bodies freed and slowly hit

The mountains. One by one, they rested. Women
Figures covered the other side of the mountains,
Hairs tugged. Heads stilled. Their arms curved
Beside their twisted legs.

These mountains became their cots
The wind their wings, and those pebbles their friends.
Their rocky cave, a cave for all the forty women,
And their fathers and mothers disappeared.

Holly Pester

Comic Timing

I went to Ilford on my own
walked up a dual carriageway
to McDonald's for a cup of tea and a think then
went back to the clinic with half a blueberry muffin
in my pocket
I was handed a white laminated
square with a number on it
I will be called by the number not
by my name I lied
on the form that asked if there was anyone
at home my Uber arrived
as the cramps started
I was told to be home within one hour
the journey time was 45 minutes
I felt nauseous
breathed slowly
the driver talked about ratings
he liked chatty and punctual passengers
he once gave a married couple no stars
when the man hit the woman
I felt dizzy we drove past his house
that's my house
he looked up my ratings and said I was
above average
you must be a nice person maybe
normally more chatty
I tried to sound lovely
said I was unwell in a weak
voice he joked I would get no stars
if I was sick
I go through my to-do list
to clean an Airbnb
I do it for money

I am a bad maid to industry's heart muscle
there was one night between guests
I had a plan lie down
with the TV on
eat a Marks & Spencer cottage pie
sleep on the sofa wake up
change the bedding
go back to the big cold house I live in and feel
treated
I knew
what to expect from
the last time the pain got
acute on a two-hour arc
I had had a hot bath
I had sat by the bath like a bird
and held
a bundle in my hand
poked about for a god or a plan
what survives a day?
but this time there was no build
up there was no flight
the pain stayed still from the clinic
to the brown
and honourable sofa
not getting easier or worse
I did not
feel anything passing through me
but the room was dark and
around me
I woke up at 7 a.m.
took some painkillers and finished cleaning
I left the key and got the bus
still bleeding a
bit still on the brink
of a big pain but going nowhere
my housemate was having a party
I was very tired but she

is out of sync and soulful
I needed to be dressed and nice
I made a bowl of beetroot
puree and hummus
I made a simple butter pastry
grated cheese
into it twisted the dough into sticks
they snapped in the oven but
smelt delicious for the people
I greeted them alone
didn't know any of them
the pain stayed still I smelt real
leaned on the counter and decided
to drink
some of my friends arrived
I behaved normally
my good friend quietly asked me
to stop being cruel to her
I was very disturbed
told her I didn't feel well
I followed smokers worried about
my good friend's feelings until
I found her in the middle
of some laughing doing
an impression of a cat
scratching a pole

her movements in a black
and white skirt
were comedic
and expert
she moved like a clown she
swung the lower half of her body
left-to-right she upped her arms
stopped to look at the room
through her hair then carried
on clowns invent new grace

for limbs out of ungraceful
lines in the room
I think I was mid-verb
like my friend I said to my head
I am mid-verb
maybe I have become the verb
I am not having
I am
abortive was the last thing I
thought before falling onto
the purple and inhabited bed
face down we have to feel
everything in our stomach
ache is tempo
I have seen millions of films
I get it
or there is no story only comedy
but my friend has clowned the time
her skirt is so stripy
I am reading it now
a difference between being
scanned for a future
or past material
for latency or tendency
I am very interested in this and I
am interested in the catch of the bed
which idea is homeless?
what is surplus connection to poetry what is the
rushed little examinations on a screen out of view
screened from me the nurse
confirms she can see a vaguer noun
something like a burn
there is not a thing but time read
translated where there might be form
it is there or a picture of noise
not like a construct
of the noise like a head it's this

way up
he is waving
creatively
at the elaborate
so it is just legibility or esoteric
reading styles
the matter
is not interpreted it is agile
easily switches between verb and noun
I could be creative but
I am beginning
to think stuck linguistically
awkward to material or reality
cannot have
have to be
timely nothing has changed
I need to find my friend
the cat the clown so
she can tell me the time
she has animation to give
I went to Ilford alone
was handed a pink laminated square
a staff was inserted I felt
hungry time was coming out slowly
I shouldn't have expected it to happen all at once
but I was told to expect it to happen all at once
they held up the staff
red for someone
I feel like a comedy
that's probably a lot of it there
it's still going on

Highly Commended Poems

Gary Allen

Technically Speaking

There were five Catholics in our engineering class –
I remember their names still
softly spoken
better dressed than the rest of us
they kept together like a flock
talked among themselves about stresses and weights
helping out on their fathers' farms

while we goofed about
goading the teachers
who knew we were too big and unruly to control
staying out all night with girls and drink
laughing as we barricaded streets
fashioning shanks in the metal workshop

and when the exams were over
and the results came out
we did no better or worse
until on the last day, when we were packing up
the classroom door opened
and the Catholic priests came among their flock
with congratulations and advice
on which Irish-American engineering-works were taking on.

Rachael Allen

Many Bird Roast

I came in, dandy and present
arguing for a moratorium on meat
of the kind splayed out on the table, legs akimbo
like a fallen-over ice skater skidding on her backside
there are dogs in the outhouse and all over the world
that we do not eat
and one small sparrow in a pigeon in a grouse in a swan
that we will certainly eat
overlooking all the drama, with as many eyes as a spider
that we'll cut in two
and the compacted layers of the various meats
will collapse away dreamily as a rainbow melts down
into the marsh where it came from
slipping meat from the bone
onto a specially designed knife
there's a call out for plates –
I'm the only one with a sense of outcry
someone says, *you weren't like this when it was broiling away*
smelling like your history, smelling like
the deep skin on your knee after playing in the sun all day
skinned with good dirt
and your under-blood just showing through
smelling like warm dry firs after burning and the outdoors
after fireworks and Novembers after tea
you eat and smell like the rest of us
dirty rat under your armpit
dirty bird in your stomach
and birds fell down the chimney with thwacks into buckets

and we got so poor we had to eat them too
strange cockatoos and once a brilliantly lit pure white dove
that we kept in a hutch with a small pot of ink
and when we let it out
it wasn't so much a raven as just a plain black dove
ready to cook, and with superstition, I learnt to.

Fatimah Asghar

Partition

you're kashmiri until they burn your home. take your orchards.
stake a different flag. until no one remembers the road that
brings you back. you're indian until they draw a border through
punjab. until the british captains spit *paki* as they sip your chai,
add so much foam you can't taste home. you're seraiki until your
mouth fills with english. you're pakistani until your classmates
ask what that is. then you're indian again. or *some kind of spanish*.
you speak a language until you don't. until you only recognize
it between your auntie's lips. your father was fluent in four
languages. you're illiterate in the tongues of your father. your
grandfather wrote persian poetry on glasses. maybe. you can't
remember. you made it up. someone lied. you're a daughter until
they bury your mother. until you're not invited to your father's
funeral. you're a virgin until you get too drunk. you're muslim
until you're not a virgin. you're pakistani until they start throwing
acid. you're muslim until it's too dangerous. you're safe until
you're alone. you're american until the towers fall. until there's
a border on your back.

Zohar Atkins

Letting Nothing Wait

Numb to the fascism of ordinary things
the reported chaos of listicles

the ambient panic of winter sky
pretending everything is fine

your hands perform their necessary
crunching while your mind runs

critical calculations. I talk to myself
about writing a poem

and the uselessness of being
clear in an age of segregated tears.

I am already aware this poem,
like perhaps every poem right now,

has
become bad –

too much tell, too political,
not enough misdirection

or else, not enough tell, too apolitical,
too much direction.

The language is coarse
like celebrity hair implants

and the private misery of fish.
Coarse and hungry, like a full belly

is full of regret
and a sharper apprehension of cosmic emptiness.

I am already aware of what a pushover I am
to be writing poems while people are out

clamoring in the televised streets
and perhaps you will love me

since you, if you are reading this,
are also likely a pushover.

Perhaps this covenant between us will serve to reinforce
our feelings of moral safety, which, we hope, are our best chance
    of payback

for a lifetime of getting kicked around by meanie-butts,
who drown out our cries with History's laugh track and claim it's
    live.

Zoë Brigley

Blind Horse Elegy

*Go after him and tell him we will give a sound horse for each
that was maimed. And tell him what kind of man did it, a man
of my mother's blood, who I cannot kill or destroy.*
                                    The Second Branch of the Mabinogi

Almost as soon as they are born, they
begin to run: the teeth in their heads
take more space than their brains,
and the eyes are the largest of all.
The mare is walking a rope around
the paddock: stamping in place: sour
muscles taut: stretched under hide:
horse stench steaming from her mane.
You didn't know how big her eyes
were when you read

the Welsh tale: *Ac yn hynny guan y dan
y meirych, a thorri y guefleu wrth y
danned udunt, a'r clusteu wrth y penneu*:
how rather than let his sister have
them (those high horses) he took
a box cutter to their lips, clipped ears
from heads, and where he could hold
them, slit their eyelids to bone. When
you talk of a horse running

perhaps you mean that as a child, you
loved your long-legged ease: the way
skin freckled with the trees:
somersaulting hills: a harras of
horses synchronous as legs: bending
and straightening in flight. How
sometimes you have ridden them:

urged them faster: thighs moving
against them: hips thrown up:
clutching. He would

cut off their tails high to the spine,
hack at their forelocks so the skin of
the forehead slips, would treat them
just as shamefully as he knows how.
Except leave them alive—still just
alive. If the tortured were blind,
there would be nothing to see: the crowd
gathered because it wanted to
watch them gurn: *ay*

*yuelly y gwnaethant wy am uorwyn cystal
a honno?* Frozen in the grass you
found an albino crow, and tried
to pick it up with gloves and trowel:
it took to its legs: half-flew into the
bush. They named you Harmless.
In a hundred years, there'll be no more
wild horses, not even on the steppes, but
tonight, with a bread knife,

he plans to carve your tail. *I will
punish you all for it. I'll take great
pleasure in it.* The crew is arriving:
the barn on fire: a last pale dawn
froths in the horse's eye.

Jericho Brown

Monotheism

Some people need religion. Me?
I've got my long black hair. I twist
The roots and braid it tight. *You're*

My villain. You're a hard father, from
Behind, it whines, tied and tucked,
Untouchable. Then comes

The night—Before I carry my
Mane to bed with me, I sit us
In front of the vanity. Undo. Un-

Wind. *Finally your fingers*, it says
Near my ear, *Your fingers. Your
Whole hands. No one's but yours.*

Nick Drake

Through the Red Light

I saw him at rush hour, courier
appearing from the primordial chaos
of the underpass into the dawn array's
thousand windscreens mirroring the sun,

on the spooky geometry of his racing bike,
cans clamped to his head, ticks on his heels,
stubble glitter-gold on his cool face,
not giving a flying fuck about red lights –

As he scanned me sideways with a passing
glance I swear I caught a shock of light,
a handful of sparks, wild fire in the pixelated
secret of his eyes – then the red turned green

but he was out of range, zigzag
zooming away as everyone gave chase

Carol Ann Duffy

Empty Nest

Dear child, the house pines when you leave.
I research whether there is any bird who grieves
over its empty nest.

                    Your vacant room
is a still-life framed by the unclosed door;
read by sunlight, an open book on the floor.

I fold the laundry; hang your flower dress
in darkness. Forget-me-nots.

*

Beyond the tall fence, I hear horse-chestnuts
counting themselves.
                    Then autumn; Christmas.
You come and go, singing. Then ice; snowdrops.

Our home hides its face in hands of silence.

I knew mothering, but not this other thing
which hefts my heart each day. Heavier.
Now I know.

*

This is the shy sorrow. It will not speak up.
I play one chord on the piano;
                        it vanishes, tactful,
as dusk muffles the garden; a magpie staring from its branch.
The marble girl standing by the bench.

From the local church, bells like a spelling.
And the evening star like a text.
And then what next...

Inua Ellams

extract from *The Half-God of Rainfall*

The year is two thousand and thirteen. Zeus' death
left a ruler's vacuum other thunder gods rushed
to fill but Sàngó, still wracked with guilt, claimed the breadth

of work fell to him. The skies over Greece could rush
and roar if he so pleased but Sàngó sought to fuse
the Gods, a cross-pantheon regime, built on trust.

Osún challenged all the Òrìṣà who, subdued
by her passion, agreed to repercussions, tough
ones too, for mortals and Gods whoever abused.

The mothers and daughters, fathers and sons shared rough
stories of their attacks. The guilty who were free
woke up to crowds chanting *Enough! Enough! Enough!*

Modupe returned all powers when the body
of Zeus was burned, but strands of god-mightiness clung
like mist around her, like rebel-song melodies.

She walked from her shrine to the river's edge where songs
that left her body, turned near waters to healing
pools, and women came to bathe in them, old and young,

from across the world. Modupe's battle-scars gleamed
in the night. Those who dared to ask how she was maimed
would be told in whispers how once she killed a king.

She joined Bolu in coaching basketball, he'd rain
The Art of War at the girls and boys. When Modupe is asked
how best to win a game, she says *Play with love. Play with pain.*

Martina Evans

Love

I couldn't help it.
I gathered cats and dogs to my chest
I love you I love you I said,
squeezing them hard
even though I knew they didn't like it.
I wanted to be gentle like Daddy – dogs' eyes swam
when he placed his crooked swollen hands on their hairy brows.
I'm back, I'm back! he shouted
as his seventeen cats poured in an unbroken pilgrimage
down the fragmented path to greet him
after any absence. They quivered
at the sound of his flat County Limerick accent
nuzzled into what he called their *vessels*
old tin lids piled up with chunks of ham, corned beef
chicken and ham roll stolen from the shop.
Feed all the birds – that was his policy,
he tossed pieces of Keating's fresh pan into the air.
Sparrow, blackbird, jackdaw, crow or pigeon,
not one bird was classified as vermin –
only the flies were a different kettle of fish.
Eschewing spray,
he favoured the quiet stickiness of fly paper:
twelve amber strips hung,
streaming from the low wood ceiling of the shop
and he moved among them like a gardener
hissing gently.

Shangyang Fang

Argument of Situations

I was thinking, while making love, *this is beautiful*—this
fine craftsmanship of his skin, the texture of wintry river.
I pinched him, three inches above his coccyx, so that he knew
I was still here, still in an argument with Fan Kuan's
inkwash painting, where an old man, a white-gowned literatus,
dissolves into the landscape as a plastic bag into clouds.
The man walks in the mountains. *No, he walks on rivers.*
The man moves among shapes. *He travels through colors.*
The mountains are an addendum of his silvergrass sandals.
Wrong, his embroidered sleeves are streaklines of trees.
None could persuade the other, as my fingers counted
his cervical spine, seven vertebrae that held up
a minute heaven in my hand. But it isn't important.
It is not, I said. It is just a man made of brushstrokes
moving in a crowd of brushstrokes. The man walks
inside himself. The string quartet of the tap water
streamed into a vase. My arms coursed around his waist.
We didn't buy any flowers for the vase. *It's ok.*
The sunlight would soon fabricate a bouquet of gladiolas.
To walk on a mountain for so long, he must desire
nothing. *Nothing must be a difficult desire.* Like the smell
of lemon, of cut pear, its wounds of snow. The man
must be tired. *He might.* He might be lonely.
He must be. The coastline of his spine, the alpine
of his cheekbone—here was where we stopped—this
periphery of skin, this cold, palpable remoteness
I held. The dispute persisted. Are you tired? *I'm ok.*
That means you are tired. *You're bitter.*
Whatever you say. If my hands departed from his skin,
the heaven would collapse. The limit remained
even though we had used the same soap, same shampoo;
we scented like the singularity of one cherry bloom.
The vase stayed empty, the sky started to rain.

My toothbrush leaned against his.
The man must be lonely, I said. *No, the mountain
is never lonely*. Burying my forehead inside his shoulder
blades, the mountain is making itself a man.

fukudapero

untitled

つたない一朝があける
幼年期が花々を揺するように
夕陽の中心一流れこむ青いガラス一けっして聞こえない音

sound | mist rises
morning trembles the flowers
like blue glass blown from sunset | an unheard

Peter Gizzi

The Present Is Constant Elegy

Those years when I was alive, I lived the era of the fast car.

There were silhouettes in gold and royal blue, a half-light in tire marks across a field – Times when the hollyhocks spoke.

There were weeds in a hopescape as in a painted backdrop there is also a face.

And then I found myself when the poem wanted me in pain writing this.

The sky was always there but useless – And what of the blue phlox, onstage and morphing.

Chance blossoms so quickly, it's a wonder we recognize anything, wanting one love to walk out of the ground.

Passion comes from a difficult world – I'm sick of twilight, when the light is crushed, time unravels its string.

Along the way I discovered a voice, a sun-stroked path choked with old light, a ray already blown.

Look at the world, its veil.

Rebecca Goss

Rachel

I spent the day being Rachel. I introduced myself as Rachel
to a stranger at the library, when we reached for the same copy
of *The New Encyclopedia of Birds*. I apologised in a way Rachel

would have apologised: prone to genuflection.
I let him take the book and wedge it under his armpit
so he could bend for his umbrella, just as I was telling him

my name was Rachel, but he turned and headed for the Loans desk.
I decided that as Rachel, I wasn't interested in birds after all,
and anyway, I didn't have a library card signed by Rachel

in black felt-pen, so I hit the big, circular button with a picture
of a wheelchair on it and waited for the doors to open fully.
I walked around the town, in rain that fell as if it was undecided

about its volume. Scant bursts would be the best way
to describe it, had someone telephoned, and after I'd said
Hello, this is Rachel speaking, told them about the weather.

Lavinia Greenlaw

The break

Deep in the dark of that year
I issued a warning. *I'm going to break*, I said
but quietly and so often that it sounded like a refrain.
People nodded and moved on. What else could they do?
Hold me? Through each and every day?
They had their own days.
One night something paused in the empty street
and tipped me sideways before moving on
and I discovered the pain I'd been trying to speak of.
I was two things now – the shocked engine
and the broken part I carried the last mile home
as if it were something I could then set down.
I met every kindness that followed with astonishment
even when they held up pictures and said
You have every reason to be in such pain.
They had looked inside me and found reasons.
To my mind, these people were gods.
I told my beloved I'd look after myself
but he kept approaching with care and patience
while I issued warnings as a form of encouragement.
There was an instant simplification of our long romance:
we spoke only of pillows, medication, tea and bread.
For months I woke beside my pain
and waited for it to knit itself to me – to become something
I carried without feeling, something incorporated
to the extent that it is not known.
Why, when I had the chance, did I not just set it down?
In what way does it complete me?

Vona Groarke

No one uses doilies anymore

so why do I hold the word to the window
so the holes in the pattern are years ago
and a visitor has come?

Impossible to talk of the mart or catarrh
as though days, clumps and clods of them,
could be glamoured by a paper doily
placed nicely on a plate.

Here, so, for this poem only,
is its wheel of stars
and star-shaped flowers

an inkling of words
as ornament,
the way stars and, yes,
flowers are.

Scott Manley Hadley

untitled

Poetry
Is a lot like sex
With a long term partner
You're not in love with anymore:
Even when it's good
It's still kinda boring

Matthew Haigh

Do You Even Lift Bro?

No   I slugged out beneath the bar
virgin under stainless steel

We have one final form
& its mouth coughs dirt clods backwards

Lads roll the glue of themselves between
their index fingers   like Bishop
when he nicked his thumb

All I see as I heft the weight
is *Alien Resurrection*

Ripley writhing in the muck of
alien intaglio   Nothing

I want to be
could be
achieved through protein

My body ideal
is a bone-white woman
louche among the brood

Robert Hamberger

Unpacking the books

They're in alphabetical order.
What better democracy?
A birdsong of Clares, rainbow of Dotys,
sextet of Gunns – paper companions
establish me through unfamiliar rooms.

I wedge my handful of pamphlets,
my own narrow volumes,
between Hacker and Hamilton. My name
tiptoes down three spines.

Will I fit here, picked from a shelf,
skimmed or discarded?
I've been told there's no competition
but hardly believe it.

A swarm of Plaths, the searchlights of Rich,
voices from a sharper conversation
I step into and aim to translate.
Who spells another language I'm greedy to hear?

Drunk on someone else's lines
I forget my new address, open books
to discover my absence, speak a phrase
for burnished pages, a word that means alone.

Nafeesa Hamid

Doctor's appointment

My mind is all woman. It is uneasy. My doctor tells me part of
my woman is ill. I don't want to woman anymore, I tell him.
He nods without looking at me. His glasses do not budge from
the tip of his nose as he continues to take notes. He asks how
long. I say since my mother birthed me and named me
Woman. He asks how long. I say too long. He says the new
tablets will help me woman again.

Rob Hindle

The Tapestry Makers of Flanders

The tapestry makers stitched a pastoral
of low fields spreading round a hill,
a stand of trees, a river's wide meandering,
a bridge to a blue-shadowed town.

Their knights flowed into battle smiling
and glib: even the dead ones beamed,
their armour as bright as the rest.
Very few fell in the fray: no-one lost.

This the official report, the wefted gloss
for approval at home, the warp well hidden
in the weave. It was never this – never
the drilled step and the pure burden

of honour: here and in every war
it is cheating and slashing and tearing
at eyes and bellies; it is whelps in a corner
spitting and shaking, terrified, dumb.

Sarah Hymas

Whale-boned Corset and Other Relics

How I loved the net flaring around my thighs,
blue smocking smoky organza
into fingertip deep slots
of mussel black nibbling my chest.
The power of an unscrutinised body.
I was the dress. And so, the loch
biting my arms as I exalt
its sting of marbled August, cutting
my fingers as they pull through
resisting cold—remote luxury
for the nicked and wrapped palms
of those girls gutting and rousing herring.
Scales tip between us—between profit and
water—between herring and cod, ploughed
with gunmetal and the slippery tongue
of empire: big fish eating little fish
eating our own cellular change.
Even the black gridlines of salmon cages
moored further up the loch
will away, on the fluke of cheap nature
which is inevitable disbelieved ignored.
To pull on this is to feel already a memory
a fraying seam of two seas colliding.

Chloë Alys Irwin

Hellingly Asylum, 1952

Before Thorazine, there was the chair
at the hairdresser.
Mabel always got a permanent wave
there, and still before Thorazine there
was the chair where
Mabel's body pulsed and drummed
against the seat
and her hair crackled to the ends with static.

> *oh boy, they've done a number on you*
says the hairdresser,
> *just look at those split ends*

Maria Jastrzębska

The Subsongs of Crow

I

Parlez-vous Kra Kra?
Pity. No one speaks
Crow these days.
Parlez-vous Caw Caw?
Ani any? *Mamy* many?
No? *No?*
If you will take the *latarka*,
I'll walk before you.
Daj mi your hand
and let's look out on a *jezioro*,
so blue *jak lód*, jak hunger.
Like ice, like *głód*.
Kocham cię till the end of

nie wiem co,
bo how to *może być*
a song *bez wron*;
with no crows? What? no
rose, not one? *bez* you?
bez końca, without end?
Which *język* is this music in?
What key are we speaking in?
I'm not *pewna, ale* –

nie jestem sure, but –
staje się
harder and harder to tell
Aż jest suddenly

neither. Ale. But, *but. Klik,*
click mistook *puk.*

You never learnt Crow?
Caw, *kra*. Oh, ah, *aaa*, o!
The End. *Koniec kreska*.
Kropka dash. Dot, *ot*. Not!

II

Dawno i daleko
once upon a when
will it be better?
When will there be
no more of these
hurtings which stop us
in our *ślady*-tracks
more than frozen breath
can tell, so that ordinary
stars and foxes can move
freely through landscapes
and uncertainties?

Once there will be
a girl or a boy or not.
Some children were always
daleko though their families
loved them yet didn't know
how to love them at all.
How could they without
warm blood? Blood
is constricted by ice
so their anger bristled
like a bear, while tears froze
for thousands of moments,

whole rivers, steel blue *jeziora*.
Once some children became soldiers,
others slaves – witnessing

wszystko or doing nothing.
But once some will become
neither. Their footprints are
right here. You may be
walking in them right now,
even if you and I don't speak
the same *język*-music.
I have only a *latarka*
but that is all you need.

III

Once upon a not exactly *ten czas*,
ten time, *tamten* time, what time?
When *las* – forest in your language –
covered the entire *kraj*
słychać było her cry, I heard it
with these mortal *uszy*-ears.
There was a lass – a *las*? Why not a lass?
Even two lasses *były* in fact.
Tu, tu lasy, albo i las.
There was a boy, who was not a boy
but a lass. And in the *śnieżny las*
oj oj! boi się, boi bo tam był ciemny las.
Are *you* afraid of the dark forest,
that's a *las*? The snowy-*śnieżny* forest?

If I lose the plot – if there ever was a *płot*
i dom with cherry trees *dookoła*.
A home, a plot, *wisienki* all around –
it's no surprise. You'd get confused
if you saw what I have seen
with my mortal *oczy*-eyes.
Za górami, za lasami, beyond the forest
and hills stood a mountain of surplus butter

when chocolate – *czekolada tak* yes *jest!*
chocolate! – was being rationed,
imagine that! If you had *widzieliście*
what I have seen, the dead on every street,
police with *pistolety* on horseback,
soldiers, tanks…

                   the snowy dark.
I've lived so long I even *pamiętam*
dawno dawno when Crows reigned
being of course *najmądrzejsze*
of all the animal queen and kingdom
(*jaki znowu dom?*) wiser
than flounder-*flondry*, braver
than all those eagly-*orły* puffing out
their feathers, who thought they had the sky –
with their sharp *igły* – sewn up.
This is the way of the *świat*, people said.
Ojoj! ale but (*but*) but
you don't have to *zaakceptować*
what's fed to you, do you?

Once upon a *dawno dawno*
when snowflakes were the size of chickens,
when wishes came true *tak naprawdę,*
as well as their own *język* everyone spoke Crow.
There was and there was not.
Kra kra, kre kre. Caw, caw, caaaaw.
People lived ever after in their own *dom* and *kraj*
or returned to their *dom* to be received
with tumultuous joy.
Wilki and lambs lay peacefully in one stall.
Wolves *i baranki* were protected alike.
Love was *miłość* and *miłość* was love
and when anyone journeyed they just crossed borders
as those *leśne ptaki*, as birds do.

IV

How do you tell   a story is a story?
Opisy are pissy!   Descriptions are boring
unless   obviously   they depict a Crow,
occasionally a *róża*   oh all right and
śnieg   Velvety   sleek   intensely brilliant
which many petalled   many feathered thing is it?
Tak   tak   yes snow   Does it have to be snow?
Icickles hang like silver bogies   from your *nos*
a turd glistens   frost-swords slice the *atmosfera*
a distant train   *daleko daleko*   smokes a path
through fields of white

                    No dobrze

skip to the *akcja*   who what   where?
But then we have to spill blood   blood
on the snow   Are you *pewna* about that?
Whose *krew*?   It's always a girl's
Not this time!   *Boi   boi się*
bo jest ciemny las   I'm
scared too   in the *śnieżny* dark
Whose blood's   on our hands?
This time   *ten czas   tamten czas*
ten sam czas   some time   same time

                    I tell you

the best is   the old woman from Lapland

frying   cloud-berry pancakes on her woodstove

That's not   in the story?   It is now
Am I in the story?   *A ja gdzie jestem?*
Of course   you're in the story
You always were   It's your story

from beginning to   *koniec kropka*   end
How does it end?
It ended   *dawno dawno* ago   Now
it's just beginning

Luke Kennard

Crow Baby

Everything plant-delicate. I'm scared to force your arms through
your sleeves. It's like trying to put a little t-shirt on a crow. That's
what it feels like. It feels like I've captured a crow and for some
reason I'm trying to show that crow unconditional love. Only it
keeps pecking me, flapping its wings and flying around the room
and into walls, completely terrified, and I'm like, come on, crow,
don't worry, I'm your father and I love you. Come and perch
on my shoulder. And the crow just flies around the ceiling like
a fan stuck on doublespeed – CAAAAAWWWWW! – stopping
only when it reaches total exhaustion. And then I'm like, I love
you. I love you, crow. I put the crow to my neck and I sit on a
metallic grey exercise ball, the volume right down and subtitles
on because love is so boring. I hum everything my dad used to
play on the piano – stuff I didn't know I remembered. Crow, I
whisper, bouncing ludicrously on the ball, I whisper what I will
whisper five years later, crouched by a drunk man weeping on
Hungerford Bridge, it's going to get better, it's going to get better
and everything is going to be okay.

John Kinsella

Milking the Tiger Snake

Fangs through a balloon, an orange balloon
stretched over a jam-jar mouth scrubbed-up
bush standard — fangs dripping what looks
like semen which is venom, one of the most
deadly, down grooves and *splish splash*
onto the lens of the distorting glass-bottom
boat we look up into, head of tiger
snake pressed flat with the bushman's
thumb — his scungy hat that did Vietnam,
a bandolier across his matted chest
chocked with cartridges — pistoleer
who takes out ferals with secretive
patriotic agendas. And we kids watch
him draw the head of the fierce snake,
its black body striped yellow. 'It will rear
up like a cobra if cornered, and attack,
attack!' he stresses as another couple
of droplets form and plummet. And when
we say, 'Mum joked *leave them alone*
and they'll go home,' he retorts, 'Typical
bloody woman — first to moan if she's bit,
first to want a taste of the anti-venom
that comes of my rooting these black
bastards out, milking them dry — down
to the last drop.' Tiger snake's eyes
peer out crazily targeting the neck
of the old coot with his dirty mouth,
its nicotine garland. He from whom
we learn, who shows us porno
and tells us what's what. Or tiger snake
out of the wetlands, whip-cracked
by the whip of itself until its back is broke.

Neetha Kunaratnam

The Afterlife

After every war
someone has to clean up. Things won't
straighten themselves up, after all
                    Wisława Szymborska,
                    The End and the Beginning

And someone will have to clean up,
but this is no job for ordinary Joes,
only specialists padded in moon boots,
face masks, and white chemical suits,

so someone will have to write a cheque
for the foreign input, the expertise
and expensive equipment:
the mine detectors and nerve sensors.

Somebody will need to order them
from the catalogue, ignore the new
solar-powered, GPS models, choose
the standard, remote-controlled breed,

as faithful and expendable as someone
sought to cordon off the area, skirt the perimeters
on tiptoe, mark out the dimensions
of the operation with sniffer dogs in tow.

Someone will need to believe the aggrieved
can make a difference, pray in numbers, petition
our leaders to subsidize farmers who can no
longer reap lest they're blown into thin air...

Someone will have to locate, then collect
any bright packages dropped after
the bombers droned off into the night,
their black boxes still replaying screams,

and someone sort out the dried food
from the prosthetic limbs, filter out the notes
of explanation, decipher a rationale
from the mistakes made in translation.

Someone will have to point out
that mustard leaves might not survive the blasts,
and checking they've turned red might set off
a barrage of blinding and a cluster of regrets.

Somebody will have to teach the children
that these M&M's aren't filled with peanuts
but pack an almighty punch. Explain that
a bomb as small as a battery can turn a sheep into a cloud.

Fiona Larkin

Rope of Sand

There is a girl next door with a sandpit.
I am a girl. I am next door. I have a sandpit too

and they match at the fence like a butterfly print.
We eye each other through gappy slats.

Mine is a slapdash scrubland, a Catholic
sandpit, a squabble of brothers. Hers, a Protestant

sandpit, a nap-time, tidy-up time, ethical
sandpit. Who's older, who's taller: we tunnel

to compare, share out my swing/her slide
her playgroup/my school, my sparkler/

her Catherine wheel, my tinsel tree/her fir.
Pale silica's ribboned with scattered earth.

*

We built something from it, something that lasted
the length of a childhood. I'd like to say

we sculpted a dolphin or at least a bridge,
a compatible lie. Yielding underfoot

but grit on the tongue, thrown in your eyes
or scrubbed on my skin, it needed surface

tension: a can of water to hold its shape,
mould an object we could both recognise.

A flood of secrets would keep it supple
until rainfall failed. It always crumpled

and in the end we rinsed our hands: each
sandpit drained out, grain by grain.

Thyrza Leyshon

Edith Sitwell

is fastening the gold collar made,
she says, *by one of my greatest friends,*
though I only met her once.
It has three pendulum blades, the largest
reaching from breast to breast.
She is taking a risk because it clanks
when reciting her poems. Tonight
she will take to The Churchill Club
a new poem, *Heart and Mind.*
It twitches among her manuscripts.

She holds her poem in jewelled fingers,
beams of light flash like searchlights finding
razor sharp partings in the hair of young soldiers.
She explains: *I've got such a dreadful cold*
and launches into *Still Falls the Rain,*
ignoring the sirens heralding an air raid.
Edith has always said of life: *it's better*
with all the banners flying – isn't it?

Although she loves jewellery, metal was dangerous
during childhood. Parents instructed
that her uselessly aristocratic nose be trussed,
prongs clamped to her face to straighten
it, her curved spine treated by iron corsets
and braces. Her favourite role is Lady Macbeth.

A doodlebug comes roaring overhead
and Edith gets louder and louder, refusing
to be silenced by an insistent missile.

On the day she dies she will breakfast
on a double martini, with the salutation: *I'm dying,
but apart from that I'm alright.*

Ada Limón

A Name

When Eve walked among
the animals and named them—
nightingale, red-shouldered hawk,
fiddler crab, fallow deer—
I wonder if she ever wanted
them to speak back, looked into
their wide wonderful eyes and
whispered, *Name me, name me.*

Theresa Lola

wikiHow To Mourn: Mourning in Healthy Ways

(1) Acknowledge your emotions in order to begin the healing process.

I am a planet orbiting a black hole/burial site/border/broken-heart
in search of a creation story where I remain alive/awake/angelic
when he leaves.

(2) Express your feelings through a tangible medium.

Take this poem as an elegy of one-sided truths
about an ended relationship.
The body is the best conductor of grief.

(3) Acknowledge that your grief is yours.

Grief is the most expensive thing I own. I hide it in a safe box,
I admit I only wear it for special occasions where men will bid
    to buy it off me.

(4) Maintain your physical health.

Before I painted my nails bright orange to make the sun jealous,
I was grey as a skinless moon, didn't shower for days,
even the walls of my room leaned in to check up on me.
My hair ate itself for lunch, left me with a bald plate for edges.
The body is feeble; negotiate with it on ways to feel beautiful
    again.

(5) Avoid using alcohol, drugs, or food to deal with your grief.

When he left I dived into glasses of wine like each one was the
    burial site
I could excavate his body from. Temporary escapes are of no use,
you are playing house with a dismantling body.

(6) Do things that you enjoy.

Watch stand-up comedy on loop, Dave Chappelle, Chris Rock,
    Kevin Hart.
Get used to laughing at how crazy a betrayed woman is,
a man's favourite joke to tell.

(7) Pamper yourself.

I gave birth to a new version of me, learning love again like
    walking.

(8) Prepare for things that may trigger your grief.

Use the mute button – pretend you chose to make them a ghost.
Of all triggers, my reflection is the most consistent.
I am reminded I should be over this by now.

Thomas McCarthy

Thigh-Bone of a Deer

The quality of sunlight. I mean the quality of light
On a morning in Iowa when you can't even remember
What you had for breakfast or even if you had
A breakfast. To float. To be young and to have broken
Free. Linden trees float above you in a lacuna
That youth has made just in time, before all of Ireland
Might have been lost to your care-worn childhood.
Coffee and the scent of cinnamon under pale leaves,
The cinnamon of Iowa City, the coffee cup
Replenished by a boy you still don't recognise as gay,
A sweetheart of a boy who misunderstood a gesture
Or a word or your ability to quote C.P. Cavafy
And all the brittle poems from a sunlit room
In Alexandria. Was Rae Delvin a boy or a girl?
How little you know of her burning, sunlit pages.
What you are thinking of is a girl with brown eyes
In a lost poem from another language, a poem
As delicate as a small boy with woman's eyes.
You are now afloat in the long American summer
After Vietnam when all of the burning issues
Became personal things. The best poets in Marvin
Bell's workshop dream of watching for fires in a forest
South-east of Seattle: they must choose, for career,
To follow Aldo Leopold's *Sand County Almanac*,
But you must choose a girl or boy fashioned from
The windswept thigh-bone of a deer. It is sunlit
Beneath these pale trees in Iowa. It is so far away
From that Irish world of wars and memoirs, from
That elderly man you knew, wearing a lemon waist-coat
And a frayed Guards tie and a scratched tank-watch
With a blue and red canvas strap. I think that man
Must have been the youth the elder loved when
He and him were very young. The housekeeper back

Home said they were both handsome but inaccessible:
I didn't know then what her tone of voice meant,
I mean her own settled and married intonation
That crackled down the line from a damp, tied cottage.
A full-size bronze of the god Hermes, a very
Expensive purchase from Artemis S.A.
Of the protector of merchants in a classical
Lysippan pose, was all the rage in the household
That summer of '78. The sculpture was
Something that defined them both, both who'd parted
Long after the housekeeper had been forsaken, and
Long before the hope of romance had returned
To Europe. That pause when Al Bowlly went silent,
Waiting for all dancers to turn and regroup
On the old vinyl that I'd rescued from among things
In a life he'd once lived, that pause of the Ray Noble Orchestra,
Seemed like the muffled 'plurp' of the Château
Lafite '45 his lover had brought and insisted they open.
In my life there were brilliant new openings:
This promise of sunlight in Iowa, all that cinnamon
And these coffee cups borne by persons whose names
I couldn't remember even then, but in his long life –
Ebbing away from me as our Pan-Am Jumbo
Banked in a holding pattern over Chicago, in his life
It seemed like the end of one long season
In Mayfair, the end of wine as deep as 20-year-old
Tawny Port; of a deep love known once, of such
A Cru; of such a compote of Cavafy, tannin and art.

Kei Miller

To Know Green From Green

And all this in a million shades of green.
James Henderson, describing Jamaica

To know the nearby bushes you must know green from green
know seafoam different from sea, teal different from tea,
& still a million shades between.

Must know hunter different from army different from rifle,
a shot fired causes birds to lift, screaming from the trees,
that 'screamin' is itself a shade of green.

Look: a parakeet, its wings bright against the night,
you must know midnight different from malachite different
from the leathery shade called crocodile.

You must know emerald different from jade; know greens that travel
towards grey – laurel, artichoke, sage. Forest is different from jungle
is different from tree which is itself a shade of green.

You must know India, Paris and Pakistan, that breeze
can rustle language out of leaves: Spanish, Persian, Russian,
& still a million tongues between.

Ciarán O'Rourke

The Cure For Nettles

Near death, his arm would quiver
down the sheets,

the blood trails tracing black
along the vein,

and when I touched I held
a cooling heat

in both my hands,
and almost choked on air

to lift his nothing-weight
so easily,

his body thin, a brittle stick
that breathed,

the transformation near-complete
from when

he stepped with dock leaves
shooting from his grip,

to hoist me from the nettle patch,
and kneel,

and reconcile
my stinging limbs with green:

milk from the fist, a water-
coloured cure.

So here, I reach for him
and flounder still,

in loss that's more an element
than ill,

his voice
the silence that remains to say,

you felt the spirit blister
through the bark

that stiffened round me
as the minutes died,

but the final fever
cleared my eyes like rain.

Morgan Parker

I Feel Most Colored When I Am Thrown Against a Sharp White Background

after Glenn Ligon after Zora Neale Hurston

Or, I feel sharp white.
Or, colored against.
Or, I am thrown. I am against. Or, when white. I sharp. I color.
Quiet. Forget. My country is a boat.
I feel most colored when I swear to god.
I feel most colored when it is too late.
When I am captive.
The last thing on my mind is death.
I tongue elegy.
I color green because green is the color of power.
I am growing two fruits.
I feel most colored when I am thrown against the sidewalk.
It is the last time I feel colored.
Stone is the name of the fruit.
I am a man I am a man I am a woman I am a man I am a
    woman I am protected and served.
I background my country.
My country sharp in my throat.
I pay taxes and I am a child and I grow into a bright
    fleshy fruit.
White bites: I stain the uniform.
I am thrown black typeface in a headline with no name.
Or, no one hears me.
I am thrown bone, "Unarmed."
I feel most colored when my weapon is I.
When I get what I deserve.
When I can't breathe.
When on television I shuffle and widen my eyes.
I feel most colored when I am thrown against a mattress,
    my tits my waist my ankles buried in.

White ash. Everyone claps.
I feel most colored when I am the punchline. When I am
    the trigger.
In the dawn, putrid yellow, I know what I am being told.
My country pisses on my grave.
My country bigger than god.
Elegy my country.
I feel most colored when I am collecting dust.
When I am impatient and sick. They use us to distract us.
My ears leak violet petals.
I sharpen them. I sharpen them again.
Everyone claps.

Sandeep Parmar

An Uncommon Language

A world gone quiet must be this fact.
For which there is no precise language.
The monitor goes off and you are led
past a succession of mothers to a room marked "empty".
Taxonomies of grief elude the non-mother,
the un-mothered, the anything-but-this-fact.
No face no teeth no eyes or balled-up fists.
To light the dark with a particular breathing.
A black lamp beats its wings ashore.

In the dark there is breathing.
After five visits to the hospital, the bruising
of inner elbows stitching themselves to themselves
in obsolescence, the nurses stop saying: *sorry for your loss.*
I may come to miss these laminated hallways.
I know my way there, to the artefact of losing.

Loosened from the factual world into a silence
where there is no grave but your own self stumbling
from floor to ceiling without an inch of your life.
Or mine. Or this particular absence.

The Lancastrian nurse is matter-of-fact.
Her metaphors are agrarian; the language of slaughter.
If you start bleeding like a stuck pig.
Under those thick white fingers an ancestry
of collapsing valves and bleating
transfigure into notes. You look familiar.
Why have you come here, again,
to my door with your metaphors of slaughter.

A folder, yellow, the word *baby*
on its cover, re-filed as miscellaneous.

What grew in you is not you but a shroud
and any idiot knows a shroud.
A ghost who wakes you up five times a night
stands undecided between rooms
shivering in its thin shadow.
I know my way here, to the language of loss.

My grandmother, who died giving birth,
explains what makes carnelian so red.
I assumed it was the iron in its veins
that made the Romans stamp their profiles
onto its brittle clots. Pulse of empire.

Don't say that / I never visited you.
A ghost is as good a family / as you may get.
Va, itni der baad thusi aaye hai?
After all this time, you've finally come?
The child that clawed you towards death is my kin.
His bones are a line pressed into the earth
you never wanted to cross, transfigured on the back
of a convoy somewhere else. It must be this fact.

DA Prince

The Window

That was my first job, he said, as we gazed
at the insignificant window. Down
the slate steps, and looking from the raised
salt-pitted pavement, where this end of town
gets hammered by the sea, it looked so small.
But sturdy, strongly-made enough to prove
that here his father fitted him with all
the craftsmanship he'd need. It wouldn't move
or crumble. Each year he'd return, to see
his work enduring. Then brought me, to know
a detail of our family history
and let this shabby mullioned window show
something inherited – that stone and wood,
well-built, can last a lifetime and go on
drawing the clean light in and doing good.
I think about it often now he's gone.

Deryn Rees-Jones

Firebird

Do you remember, Julia, that night,
you found me on Lon Pobty without keys?
Midnight, drunken midnight, stars broken, the moon –
old battered, shiny, word-enamoured friend.
We were 18, 19, 20. Nobody really counted
years or days. Glow worms, fireflies, the
liquefaction of your clothes…
We could make an evening of it yet.
Kingfishers, dragonflies.
Someone had painted lines from Auden
on the college car park. I shadowdanced with hands
across your flat's white walls.
You pulled *The Firebird* from its record sleeve,
strangest of choices! And so the room caught fire.
Your eyes which I could never
place a colour for in English –
glas – became the music, blasted out. The dancers
danced in Kaschkei's garden. The bird's wings shook.
Scarlet oriole? Goldfinch? Its song of 33.3
across the turntable a glorious span
of blazing flames. Words lit us up.
The century slipped back and shocklike flames
cried out *What I do is me: for that I came.*
The torturer's horse
kept scratching its beh —.

*

Time deepens: in its nets, the fishgasp loss
just keeps on happening.
Your blood cells sicken. Leaves
empty from the trees.

We text back and forth in darkness.
Little hand held world of light
and frequencies. What stepping in
and back and on
is this, this middle age?

*

Dear friend, sometimes I lose myself. The mind's embodiedness
the wounded day's. I wait for bridging light, the early hours.
Life happens. So we step across the hours, notice our visitations.
Lost threads – days like cuts, electric wires, barbed wire and glass –
cliché we learn, routine in daily repetitions. End
and start, delay – our offices. A child's bleak nightmares
speak the early hours. I might think of a whole day, haunted,
looking back, as something that I walk towards.
Well, let us all walk into that morning where a room
might hold one remnant of the phoenix's flight, its rage.

Sophie Robinson

FUCKING UP ON THE ROCKS

ducking my head under each wave on fire
island i try to think of other times ive felt this done
w/life & survived
frank o'hara died here everybody knows
alcoholics die everywhere all the time everybody knows
he was purple wherever his skin showed
       i never thought of myself as a useless drunk
             i never felt
so unspecial   *through the white hospital gown*
in the daytime it feels
like it would be easy to die
to dip my head under
          just a second too long
             but in the dark death is real
    like an animal up close
                  he was a quarter larger than usual
on the edge of sleep you could fall
straight into & thru it   & nobody wld know yr name there
naked in the atlantic at midnight cutting a path where the moon hits
the water i could swim a straight line out into forever & nobody
would stop me. would know my name. *every few inches*
there was some sewing composed
of dark blue thread i want to shut my eyes i want to shut a million
   things
strawberry moon   orange to silver   my simple tits
bobbing on the water   *some stitching was straight and three or four*
inches long   others were longer and semicircular   urge to die
   breathing out & folding in
on itself until it feels like nothing   we get out   shiver   lose the keys
   to the house
find them & laugh on the porch   *the lids of both eyes were bluish black*
   jameson

drinking an inch of mezcal & me sucking on my seltzer like it's a
  beer
alive   smiling   only half-quitting   only half-gone   a normal
  heart
flashing in & out on the shore *it was hard to see his beautiful*
blue eyes which receded a little into his head   the wifi is out
my 4g is fake   replacing each image in my recent life with a
  square and a ?
(i know rite)   *he breathed with quick gasps. his whole body quivered.*
                        i have taken a solemn vow to stop looking
at your face on the internet   to stop imagining your unkind
  thoughts
                                of me   my life as a little nobody
there was a tube in one of his nostrils down to his stomach
i go to sleep in a wood-panelled room the same length & width
as my bed   & count the waves as they break
over my head   i sleep like im already dead
                        face to the wall
greedy for the nothing   won't fall
in the crib he looked like a shaped wound
i wake up constipated
in the morning sun   drink coffee & smoke
on the beach feeling full of shit   & good to no-one
his leg bone was broken and splintered and pierced the skin
every rib was cracked.
a third of his liver was wiped out by the impact
i could make a home here prone forever
belly to the sand
let my messages go unread
let my phone battery run flat
let the sun burn my back
let all the ships fuck up on the rocks
indistinguishable   baby small   little pieces
floating   like the world floats   gay   unbroken
bloated & golden
a monument to my favourite alcoholic
the greatest homosexual   who ever lived & died

Maria Sledmere

Ariosos for Lavish Matter

1.
My self a disc I can't compact. Instead relay anecdotes
about the cost of waitressing in several nocturnal
glistenings; remember it was Coleridge
who could not walk because of hot milk
so my shame is a migraine deprived of opiates
and mostly I unravel my uniform
steaming beneath the lindens.

2.
In profile much prettier, every epoch
has its scary techne. Dream where my mother
reapplies lipstick in the restaurant mirror
and my life is the tiniest violet smudge at the edge.
Customers fill the sepulchral dark as other shadows
tuned to mystery, clearly
in pain with better quality, keep warm.

3.
Resisting the hot mathematics of football
downward to HD and popcorn memories, hum
of love and bike wheels. Honeycomb crunched
in the back of my mouth like a birthday.
These splintering words
to be dressed and buried, most of human
and more. A scalp massage is tentacle pleasure.

4.
Shouldn't we pick kin that resist us?
Dreadfully expensive, the wristwatch future
of light that lets in, silver fingers
threatening piano wires to whiter fire.

Tweets excepted, the lure of the bright
and Maytide familiar; remember he was
supposed to come play but didn't and hurt.

5.
An empathic blue sky, little organ donation
around the rain. In the red, the muscular
cumulus news fell away. Meat that thins
without freezing. I don't want to look
the way, this way. Cashing misery
for Mercury, cash in gin. Two cold halves
of a decent cut, fail to function as ritual.

6.
Hypothetical rhymes halo the bay,
become powder. How are we now.
The camera lifts the wax from your eyelids
startling a blankness of planetary lashes.
No sweet work of skin was sufficient,
those silhouette girls with faraway poses.
Switch off the desert, I'm not listening.

7.
Rub my eyes around the fantasy cedar
as if the sap stopped happening.
Hydraulic thought as all the rage
and wasting, most citizen damage
dismisses the winterized lanterns.
One line follows the next, a nest
curling up tight the language of saplings.

8.
In crispest best, street clover pales
to lilac assets; too true of an elevator birth
between ages. Starved in the dark
the poem's gloaming is a hollow in the elm

of my belly, not to sprawl any longer
the vitamin lore of extroversion. I require
such luxury of inherited messages.

9.
So maybe Meredith's hereditary spells
crested the gleaning sea's chartreuse, reductress
of cool semesters. Exceptionally latent
the corridor of aesthetic residues
repainted a glorious yellow.
All premonitions ring with red:
a seagull eating a seagull.

10.
Interrupted outlook is late-night, tricyclic
opening your mailbox for ravens. Advertise
a fresh electronic duo, treat us confidentially:
our slick new remix made the radio.
This addiction can wait till Friday, as I add
to my nerves undigested iron. No condition.
Popping kelp didn't help, am I yet shining.

11.
Halfway to Brunswick and back
in lossy compression of monochrome era. Missing
you much in abandoned houses, cloistered green.
Nothing a shake of desiccated opals won't fix
when the sparkler goes, death as fizz and cravings.
Some sort of wartime cousin now a chocolatier
and I really don't know what to say
ready salted with these read receipts.

12.
My womb through the night was shredding
to suffer the sheets as glass
and the body's luminosity, I'd say

the wrought metallic twang of the tongue.
I pay for everything
and the recipe stays central
to rich boys, coke and brand new menus.

13.
Can I fetch you anything while I'm here?
How was it this time. The cervical curve
of bone at the brink of the plate, a balance
I exact as gravity. What sorts of eternity
do we choose for our labour?
I was so afraid of orange, poverty; your eyes
if they opened just so, like beautiful eggs.

14.
It didn't take long to recreate
the opaque catatonia of sad hospitality; news of aniseed
drained the pool. No-one came.
Chalked up to biospheric sequence
and now receding. Is there bread with that.
I spent ten minutes sketching to change things.
Remember you can always sleep.

15.
Didn't I say a dairy-free dream
would deliver me strange to some home or another.
When everything grew too green
and the smell of the bluebells
still deep in your neck like a song.
A sort of Gaussian moment propels me, lullaby ever
of red-berried February, the alkaloid.

16.
Coltan imbues each blade
of archival lust upon airplanes. A touch.
Some other pixelated dryad could tell

time from the web of a spider; my primary
accent dissolved as sand then ambient.
Each window of night became complicated,
pasteurised. I could not acquire the nascent tinder.

17.
Fluorescence rises from the woods
to a clearing of gilded tips, expiry dates, essays.
These demented lands where I love you
in the drafted webpage, a fractal
synapse unsampled. Our hours as baskets
of moulding fruit, glitching seeds. This can happen.
I like the loops of your voice, dust, the trivial starlings.

Austin Smith

American Glue Factory

for Rachel Carson

All your childhood you watched
Old horses file up a wooden ramp
Into the American Glue Factory
And file out as smoke.
This was in Springdale, Pennsylvania,
Up the Allegheny from Pittsburgh,
In the early part of the twentieth century.
Though it was never mentioned, you knew
What the horses were being turned into.
In your desk at school was a bottle
You used to join this and that
To this and that. You knew horses
Were what hung the gold and silver
Stars in the firmament of your notebook,
What made the hearts stick
In the valentine you never gave
That girl at school. Summer nights
The stench of burning
Horses drove you into the house
From the screen porch where you sat
Reading about the sea.
It was there you first learned that
Something in the air can close a story.

Jean Sprackland

April

machine of spring with all your levers thrown to max
clouds in ripped clothes and sheep trailing afterbirth
where last week's buds sucked blue juice from the dusk
now the branch is swollen   priapic
cherry bling and hawthorn sex-bed smell
motorway hedgerows on thrust   electric rapefields

your levers are jammed and nothing can pull them back
not now   not frost   not squall
city gutters clogged with blossom
muddy ponds spuming with cannibal tadpoles
the long blinding days   your bashed clock
the violent small hours   magpie clacking at the robin's nest

and us lying open-eyed all night
breathing in the green noise of pollen
hearing the long bones of the trees stretch and crack
wondering   will you ever power down or is this it now
wondering   what can any death amongst us mean to you
and will we make it through to summer or is this it now

Julian Stannard

Eau Sauvage

For Charles

Richard John Bingham, 7th Earl of Lucan (born 18 December 1934; presumed
dead), commonly known as Lord Lucan, was a British peer suspected of murder
who disappeared in 1974.

I get an unexpected
text from Lord Lucan:

Will you read my poems?
Yes, Lord Lucan, I will.

Tomorrow, when I look
for the message it isn't

there – I mean his part
of the message isn't there.

Just, Yes Lord Lucan I will.
It sounds like a song.

Yes, Lord Lucan, I will.
Yes, Lord Lucan, I will.

A week later a package
drops through the letter box –

22 Landguard Road
into a communal hallway,

full of envelopes
addressed to neighbours

who've long since disappeared:
Miss Moon, Miss Pinkerton

Miss Reckless, Miss Raven
and the loveliest of all

Miss Craven.

I read the poems
with trembling lips.

I read the poems
with trembling thighs.

I read the poems
with widening eyes

and then ring Charles Boyle
ex-poet of Shepherd's Bush.

Is that Charles Boyle
ex-poet of Shepherd's Bush?

Yes, says Charles
as – indeed – you well know.

I want to find the right *ton*

I want to suggest
in a previous life

that I rubbed shoulders
with interesting people.

A little hushed, throaty, I say,
The poems of Lucan have landed.

What are you talking about?
says Charles, are you demented?

I think you should take a look.
I think you should publish the book.

Actually, I rather enjoy thinking
of Charles Boyle in Shepherd's Bush.

Charles says, Read me a couple,
read me a poem by Lucky Lord Lookey.

Read me, read me. Alright, *alright*.
I'm sifting through the poems

and the room is zinging with
the aroma of *Eau Sauvage*

Read me a couple, read me a couple.

I'm reading them to myself.
I'm not reading them to Charles.

I'm reading them to myself.
They're so louche and so elegant

so decadent and so intelligent.
In fact they're not poems at all.

They're too good to be poems.
It's like putting one's hand in a glove.

It's like smoking a little Tina
Bonjour little Tina. Bonjour.

They're not poems at all.

Poems which are better than poems
ought to be called something other

than poems. Read me a couple
says Charles, read me a couple of poems

that are better than poems.

Charles is making a strange noise
at the end of the phone.

I have the most extraordinary
non-poems in the world

and Charles is making a noise
at the end of the phone.

The ex-poet of Shepherd's Bush
the most insouciant publisher

in the city of London
the most audacious publisher

in the city of London
the most charming publisher

in the city of London
is making a strange noise

at the end of the phone

Oh read me a couple.
Oh read me a couple.

No! No! No!

And then I pretend
someone's knocking

at the door.

In fact I go to the door
and start knocking on it

knock, knock, knock:
Charles, I say, someone's knocking

at the door – You'd better
answer it, he says.

I think he might be thinking
it's Lovely Lord Lucky.

Knock, knock, knocking
at the door.

Who's knock knock
knocking at the door?

Virginia Woolf.
Miss Photo-Synthesis.

Frederick Seidel.
Charles Manson.

Charles Boyle.
Not even Charles

can be in two places
at the same time.

Professor Kiss.
Miss Reckless.

Arthur Rimbaud
with only one leg.

Salvador Dalí
Lord Lucan,

alleged killer of Nannies,

holding some
lead pipe and

a mediocre bottle
of vodka.

Oh Lord Lucan

is knocking at the door!
(Obviously he isn't,

I'm putting on a
show for Charles!)

Hang on a moment, I say
walking round the room

in a euphoric circle.
Hang on a moment, I say

walking round the room
in a euphoric circle.

Sweet Lord – sweet Lord
someone *is* knocking

at the door!

I mean someone
who is not me –

someone who is not me!

The jazz police are leaning
on my shoulders.

The Poetry Foundation
is going through my folders.

Blah, blah de blah
                    blah

Charles is making a strange noise
and someone's knocking at the door.

And I have seen enough
black and white films

to know that the person
in the shit – which happens to be me

(how did that happen?)

needs to be fleet of foot
and I would be happy

to flush the poems – I haven't
yet thought of another name –

for the poems other than *poems* –
down the lavatory:

the flusher is a spitter
rather than a flusher

the flusher is a spitter
rather than a

I called the plumber
a hundred times.

His name is Trevor.
Oh, he's subtle.

I called the plumber
a hundred times.

I know he's there

at the end of the phone
feigning a psychotic attack

in the back of his van.

You can stick your little pins
in that voodoo doll.

I cannot flush
the Lucan poems.

I cannot burn the Lucan poems
not a log in sight.

OPEN UP! OPEN UP!

Lord Lucky has written
his poems on exquisite

parchment and I realise now
I will have to eat them.

That's what they do in France
when the Gestapo comes

knocking on the
                              door.

The young woman who
everybody loves drinks

a glass of Beaujolais

and swallows the name
of the agent which slips down

her throat

and lies in the pit of her stomach.
We know the Gestapo

will not break her –
they will torture her

and they will kill her.
She will die, having

swallowed the name

of a very important agent.
She will save France.

They will not break her.
There will be a statue of her

in Rue Julien-Lacroix
Je ne regrette rien/ everything.

I am now eating the poems
of Lord Lucan

what a pity he wrote so many!

The Gestapo are knocking
at the door

and I am eating the poems
of Lord Lucan.

Eat eat eat.
Eat eat eat.

And I say – in a muffled voice
I'm coming! I'm coming!

Give me some extra moments
Meine Herren

I'm just getting out of the shower!
As if.

I called the plumber
a hundred times.

Maybe I should pretend
I am merely a piece of paper

and rustle, rustle
or maybe I should just lie doggo

for a while –

I'M COMING! I'M COMING!

I don't want the Gestapo
to think I'm some

dirty, un-washed poet
floating on the Oh là là

of drug-fuelled auto-erotica

so I'm dabbing
my neck with *Eau Sauvage*

and slipping on
the silkiest of dressing gowns

as if I'd just been putting
the final touches to

Blithe Spirit

Dabbing on a little *Eau Sauvage*.

Eat eat eat.
Eat eat eat.

I'm coming! I'm coming!

Rebecca Tamás

WITCH FIRE

the witch lay in immense thick darkness
around her were the bones of the body
she burned
let be burned and slipped off snakelike
being witch the witch still breathed
under the pile of logs and ash
at the corner of what should be known
adjunct to her bones are the other bones
adjunct to her skin are the other skins
and other hair and other eyes hard globules
what dead thoughts can live down here
someone didn't like her husband
someone loved hers and screamed to be separated
someone kept their own shed of goats which they
tended like children someone read philosophy
someone had a tic where they kept scratching
their face someone had had a recurring dream
that they were a medieval knight with clean
gilt armour and their own horse and castle
who rode out on adventures and would
drive through the thicket branches slapping their
face find a damsel tied up against a tree with
long wavy brown hair and when they got close
would see that they are the damsel they are the horse
they are riding themselves they are saving themselves

the witch is tired and at war
she hates the past and she hates the present
she hates how easy it is how innocuous how boring
hates England and wants to stop at that but finds
herself hating them all she hates the landmasses of
Europe their fat seas their pin-tip hills she hates
their verdant grasses and their polite architecture

their binaries their sinewy rivers their flatlands and mud and
     windmills
and factories and press organisations and colonial bureaucracy
     and prisons
and fellowships and barnyards and pump rooms and lochs and
     silage plants
there is light and she loves it coming in from space
clean and sharp as an equation light slipping under chapped eyelids
sometimes warm sometimes cold hint of blue roughness
of spectral red twist of lilac blue rim spot of green
the witch can love light unexpected the witch can feel it
gathering up in itself the light is not stupid or clever
the light is an option as yet unplanned
unknown

Adam Thorpe

Chinooks

They would press their ears hard to the ground
'for the warning', she says: bright-eyed behind
black-rimmed glasses, essaying her English.

Her grandfather's generation, now: he fought
for the Vietcong. For the Revolution!
So whenever the Americans came

the villagers were hiding 'in the earth', below.
She's staring out at the glassy breakers
with their scrolled-back foam, gunmetal grey

beneath a clouded sky. 'You've read of China
wanting our sea?' 'Of course.' 'Why can't we
Vietnamese just be keeping what is ours,

our sea, our land?' I babble something about
global strategy, the schemes, the scrabbles
of history as the balmy, tropical air blows in,

indifferent either way. 'I suppose rotors
are very loud,' I conjecture, and mime
the twirl of the blades. 'They couldn't *hear*,' she says,

'they were too far away!' (The vibrations, stupid.)
'They *sensed* it,' I suggest. 'They sensed it
through the ground.' Like a distant train

singing in the rails. She nods. The conical hats
were bobbing about in the paddy fields as they always
will, the Chinooks like grotesque insects looming

over the hills too late to operate
their deadly chatter. What will it take for people
to bend down to the ground and hear? No,

not hear, for as she said it wasn't the whumps
of the rotors that alerted them, but the motion
in the air, the vibrations, the shift and knock

of the pressured soil, the fluid molecules,
the belonging to her people of the broken land.
Its hurt, its crying out, *Beware, beware,*

the Chinooks are on their way! We wouldn't have
a clue what was coming, now … deaf to the earth
and upright as we are, our hands brushed clean

of saving soil, and the wind already turned.

RA Villanueva

Namesake

For Jacob Sam-La Rose

By daybreak the two had been locked
together for hours on the riverbank
among reeds and moss flowers,
struggling, some translations say,
or *grappling*, knuckles braided,
wrists bruised, their bodies become
a dovetail joint where a windpipe
might disappear in the glow
and salt of a bicep. Choke hold,
half-nelson, laughter and necks'
crack and parry – imagine the funk
and rumble of their waltz:
that Jacob vs. his God, or vs.
the face of his God; or that
Jacob folding into a stranger's
outstretched wings, the story,
as ever, ending in blessings
and one hip pulled clean
from its socket. Such is the algebra
of certain parables that we
can cast other rivals
for the fray: this Jacob
fighting his faith or yes, *wrestling*
the spectres of fatherhood; this
Jacob and the flare of Peckham
street lamps, staring-down
train tables and yet another sunrise
just north of home; Jacob chasing
invoices from the Queen,
or bike thieves making-off
with new wheels; this Jacob's flex

against the bindings of language,
of acronyms, of history, of
how boys too often worship fists
instead of syllables, or
the weight of a lover's heart
in their hands. In Gauguin's
Vision after the Sermon, perhaps
what matters most isn't the soft
knot of blue in the upper
reaches of the canvas, or
the staggering radiance
of the field where Jacob and
what we take to be an angel
seize each other, but
a gathered congregation,
their faces lit by what promises
to crack Jacob open,
but never does, their eyes
shut, humbled by calamity
and its tenderness, sure now
that they know: devotion,
what it means to praise, to love,
to survive love and the divine.

Rebecca Watts

Red Gloves

The women are carrying the coffin. Under the fear
of slippage they make slow steps.
We cannot say that they advance.

More than one woman is weathering, from the cool
top of her head to her strained fingers to her toes
pushed together in interview shoes, the urge,
like a rip tide, to run backwards and away.
Today is not a normal day.

How awkward we are:
even were they to confer it would not be possible
for these four women to set down their load
with elegance. The military could manage it –
but military is system, control from above.

The women are moving from within.
More than one of them will go to ground today.
More than one will be yanked
otherwards. Husbands and children.
How requiring, how embarrassable we are.

One is wearing red woollen gloves. She is pressing them
to the wicker as though without her hands' small force
the entire construction would fold outwards.

Hugo Williams

Shadow Pack

Business as usual?
The same again, landlord?
The mixture as before?
Or is everything different
now that everything exists
in a shadow pack?
I think about Portugal sometimes,
as if it were still there.

Either I draw the curtains
shutting out the light,
or I draw the curtains
letting in the night.
When the moon lays
two sheets of writing paper
on my bedroom floor,
I dwindle south in a sort of boat.

I'll never forget
the eager doing of nothing,
rolling it into balls
and placing them on shelves
the way we used to at the office.
I don't go there any more,
for I have gained
a poor understanding of time.

It darts about the place
in a pattern of lightning flashes:
a piebald, then a skewbald face,
expressing horror.
From a certain angle
it looks like a pantomime horse.

I turn it inside out
in case there is happiness in it.

I don't feel so confident
when a little broken shadow
creeps into my room.
I wonder what's the matter
with 60 watt bulbs these days.
They don't seem to light up
the way they used to.
I put it down to faulty wiring.

Alison Winch

Bishop Berkeley is My Boyfriend

A mind at liberty to reflect on its own observations, if it produce
nothing useful to the world, seldom fails of entertainment to itself.
Bishop Berkeley

You think I'm joking. He's a spit of the portraits,
right down to his unbaked baked bean head and black
    stick-on eyebrows.
He wears puffy-ruffle sleeves that billow just-so by his
    waterfall-cum-fountain.
Not that I've met him! Our dirt is done via carrier pigeons
born in the gin lanes of the historical metropolis.

There's no need to actually bone: a typical epistle from his
    authentic quill.
You saucy maid, are as vivid as wifey
lying here in the sensory impression of our marital bed.
(Can he be married if he's a bishop?
There's so much I need to learn.) *Darling, all that matters*
    are Ideas.

He explains the body parts to suck and push himself into;
    my passive qualities.
It's hornier than it sounds! But also worse.
The pigeons always hammered *tok-tok*-ing at my double-
    glazed suburban window
even when I'm teaching in the morning.
It's hard work being fuckable. Or maybe it's hard work
    being fake.

Ann Wroe

At San Damiano

With his heart already completely changed ... he was walking one day by the church of San Damiano near Assisi, which was abandoned by everyone and almost in ruins. Led by the Spirit, he went in to pray and knelt down devoutly before the crucifix. Then ... with the lips of the painting, the image of Christ crucified spoke to him. 'Francis,' it said, calling him by name, 'go and rebuild my house; as you see, it is all being destroyed.' Francis was like a man out of his senses ... but pulled himself together to obey ...

From that time on, compassion for the Crucified was impressed into his holy soul, and the wounds of the Passion were stamped deep in his heart. He could not hold back his tears ... but went through Assisi begging for oil to fill the lamps in San Damiano.

Celano, *Remembrance of the Desire of a Soul* 1, vi, viii

'In pictures of God and the Blessed Virgin painted on wood, God and the Blessed Virgin are honoured ... yet the wood and paint ascribe nothing to themselves, because they are just wood and paint. ... So the servant of God is a kind of painting ... that is, a creature of God who can ascribe nothing to himself.'

Francis in *Scripta Leonis*, 104

'Most High and Glorious God, enlighten the dark place of my heart.'

Prayer of Francis before the crucifix of San Damiano

You come to kneel in penitence.
Here is the tree. Here is your Lord
nailed up like some corn-stealing bird,
eyes dulled, wings splayed. Thin streams of blood
run scarlet from His feet and hands.
You're crying now. You're crying now.

It is an image done on wood.
That's all. Yet through your falling tears
He trembles into light, Who sent
these tears to you. Half-conscious sighs
that leave your lips now breathe from His,
incense and words, His name and yours,

and you who were mere paint and wood,
a senseless thing, begin to feel
love-notes that stir within your spine
and shiver upwards, tuning you
to bliss or agony like His
against the grain, against the grain,

then as new buds swell through the bark
like oil in spring, chill sweat breaks out
on His brow, yours, till your dead wood
turns soft as His, and you leap up
full-leafed towards that blazing grace—
The nails are sharp in His embrace.

San Damiano, April

At last at San Damiano the storm broke,
flushing the roads to rivers. On our right

a handmade sign stood propped beside a stall,
Vendesi olio nuovo: not a sight

expected at this season of the year,
or in such weather. Maybe it was old;

it had that look; or maybe it referred
to pressings never-ending, to the cold-

crushing of new-crop sainthood, over there
in that dark vault sunk in an olive grove,

obscured by windscreen-wipers in the rain:
from bruising wood, gold welling drops of love.

Before this tree
split
lightning deep,
a stream
keeps silence,
and the birds
also

Biographies of the shortlisted writers

Forward Prize for Best Collection

Fiona Benson (b. 1978 Wroughton) says that the terrifying sequence of Zeus poems that form the first half of *Vertigo & Ghost* emerged from 'a long buried experience, and then a sudden pouring-in of words, that I can only explain as coming out of the woods'. The sequence makes palpable the sexualised violence latent in Greek mythology, with Zeus as abuser-in-chief, abetted and feared. It is followed by an exploration of the complex and ambivalent terrain of early motherhood.

Benson's debut collection, *Bright Travellers*, was shortlisted for the 2015 Forward Prize for Best First Collection and received great critical acclaim. Ben Wilkinson described how she 'treat[s] the poem as a kind of secular prayer', and indeed many of the works in *Vertigo & Ghost* arrive at prayer as their end-point: the last words of 'Eurofighter Typhoon', the final poem in the collection, are 'Mary, Mother of God, have mercy, mercy on us all.'

Niall Campbell (b. 1984 South Uist) published his first collection, *Moontide*, a month after the birth of his son: the poems in *Noctuary* (a journal of the night hours) were written in whatever moments he could snatch from the larger responsibilities of parenthood. 'The world, I think, seems larger in my first collection, while in this book it is often just the size of a dark room,' he writes.

One of the inspirations for *Noctuary* was the *Elegies* of Douglas Dunn: as Dunn's work is a book of 'love strewn through with sadness', Campbell envisaged his own poems as being animated by love intermingled with 'the hope, the tenderness and the exhaustion' of being a father. He lives in Leeds, and is currently collaborating on an opera with the composer Anna Appleby.

Ilya Kaminsky (b. 1977 Odessa, in the former Soviet Union, now Ukraine) has described how, 'for a refugee, there is a beauty in falling in love with a language'. His first poems were written in Russian; after his family emigrated to the USA in 1993, Kaminsky chose English because 'no one in my family or friends knew it – no one I spoke to could read what I wrote. It was a parallel reality, an insanely beautiful freedom. It still is.'

Deaf Republic, Kaminsky's second collection, is a modern fable or parable; in an unnamed country, a deaf child is killed by soldiers dispersing a protest, and the town falls sympathetically deaf in response, coordinating their dissent via sign language. 'This silence is personal,' writes Kaminsky. 'I did not have hearing aids until I was sixteen and my family immigrated. As a deaf child, I experienced my country as a nation without sound. I heard the USSR fall apart with my eyes.'

Vidyan Ravinthiran (b. 1984 Leeds) started work on *The Million-petalled Flower of Being Here* with no intention of publishing it. 'I began writing sonnets to my wife, privately – they were genuinely for her ears only,' he says; it was only in the middle of the sequence that he began to realise that it might be of interest to other readers.

Ravinthiran is a senior lecturer in North American literature at the University of Birmingham and an editor of the online magazine *Prac Crit*. *The Million-petalled Flower of Being Here*, which takes its title from a line in Philip Larkin's poem 'The Old Fools', is his second collection; his debut, *Grun-tu-molani*, was shortlisted for the Forward Prize for Best First Collection and the Seamus Heaney Prize.

Helen Tookey (b. 1969 Leicester) takes inspiration from the fleeting and vestigial – dreams, overheard stories, works of art and remembered children's book illustrations all contribute to the eerie landscapes of *City of Departures*. There is also a strong European dimension, with poems set in Germany, Denmark and France: part of the overwhelming sense of loss arises from Brexit and the consequent ruptures of place and identity.

Tookey lives in Liverpool, where she works as senior lecturer in creative writing at Liverpool John Moores University. Her previous collection from Carcanet, *Missel-Child*, was shortlisted for the Seamus Heaney Prize. The poems she is currently writing arise out of her response to the ecological crisis: poetry, she says, can and should tackle big ideas, 'but you've got to get those ideas across by showing the reader something specific and tangible that they can take hold of'.

Felix Dennis Prize for Best First Collection

Raymond Antrobus (b. 1986 London) has been writing poetry for as long as he can remember. 'I had permission to engage with it without the baggage that many people in the UK have, where poetry is solely associated with some negative experiences in English lessons at school,' he writes. 'I associate it with family and songs and solitude.' The poems in *The Perseverance* (taking its title from a London Fields pub) are as personal as solitude and as universal as songs: they include elegies for Antrobus's father, explorations of d/Deaf experience and meditations on growing up Jamaican-British.

Antrobus is a freelance teacher, and one of the first six graduates of Goldsmiths' MA in spoken word education, as well as one of the inaugural Jerwood Compton Poetry Fellows, and the second poet in residence at the London Book Fair. His advice for younger poets is to be bold in their dislikes: 'There is no holy grail of poetry, no matter what a school curriculum or university reading list tells you. Trust the things you connect with and grow from there.'

Jay Bernard (b. 1988 London) is an archivist and filmmaker as well as a poet, and the poems in *Surge* bring an archivist's eye and a filmmaker's technique of pacing to bear on their radical excavation of black British history, drawing lines between the New Cross Fire of 1981 (in which 13 young black people were killed) and the contemporary legacy of racism and neglect which culminated in the Grenfell disaster. What place in the archive can there be for the lack of accountability and closure, the body and its wounds? Bernard gives a partial answer in 'Ark': 'I file it under fire, corpus, body, house.'

'In one way, the most important poems [from *Surge*] are the voices from beyond, because those are the ones that invite the audience in,' writes Bernard. 'In another way, the more important poems are the ones I read less often. The quiet ones that document commemorations, small moments, people I have known, notebook fragments.' In 2018, Bernard won the Ted Hughes Award for *Surge: Side A*, produced by Speaking Volumes and first performed at the Last Word Festival.

David Cain (b. 1972 Luton) found his interests in poetry, social history and sporting history being drawn together when a poem of his about the agony of watching Luton Town lose at Wembley was read on national radio, and he was invited by the club to contribute a regular poem to the match-day programme. His debut, *Truth Street*, explores a darker part of the same territory; published to mark the thirtieth anniversary of the Hillsborough disaster, it is a collage of eyewitness statements from the second inquest in 2014.

'There was a real humanity and indeed beauty in those words,' writes Cain, who modelled his process on Charles Reznikoff's *Holocaust*. 'I wanted to try and rescue those lines from all the fragile jargon, and also the headline news verdicts.' *Truth Street* was first performed in its entirety at the Utter! Lutonia festival in 2017.

Isabel Galleymore (b. 1988 London) was the first poet in residence at Tambopata Research Centre in the Amazon rainforest. 'The opportunity to encounter different types of creature – spider monkeys, pink-toed tarantulas, caiman – was irresistible,' she writes, and many of the poems in *Significant Other* display the fruits of that opportunity. Another residency in Cornwall gave her the opportunity to make a close study of local rock pools, and the collection is liberally dotted with sonnets about bivalves and barnacles, including the magnificent spiny cockle which gives the book its cover illustration, 'let[ting] / its long pink foot slip like a leg / from the slit of its crenulated skirt'.

Galleymore works as a lecturer in creative writing at the University of Birmingham; her poetry appeared in Carcanet's *New Poetries VII* anthology, and in a pamphlet from Worple Press, *Dazzle Ship*. She is currently working on a new pamphlet of prose poem fragments, tentatively titled *Cyanic Pollens*.

Stephen Sexton (b. 1988 Belfast) spent a lot of time when he was nine years old playing Super Mario World. *If All the World and Love Were Young* remaps the pastoral tradition onto the familiar Nintendo landscapes; like Milton's 'Lycidas' it is a pastoral elegy, in this case for the poet's mother. He began work on the sequence in 2015, and in his own words 'soon realised that this particular game was so much a part of my childhood that I couldn't write about it without thinking of my childhood, and I couldn't write about my childhood without thinking of grief'. But the poems, like the best pastorals, still retain a real sense of freshness and wonder, well summarised by the collection's familiar epigraph: 'It's a-me, Mario!'

Sexton's first pamphlet, *Oils* (Emma Press), was a Poetry Book Society Pamphlet Choice; he won an Eric Gregory Award in 2018. He lives in Belfast, where he teaches at the Seamus Heaney Centre for Poetry.

Forward Prize for Best Single Poem

Liz Berry (b. 1980 Black Country) won the Forward Prize for Best
Single Poem in 2018 with 'The Republic of Motherhood', having
previously won Best First Collection in 2014 for her Chatto debut
Black Country. 'Highbury Park' describes an overgrown park in
Birmingham where Berry went on long walks with her newborn son.
'As the spring came I felt my body being brought slowly back to life by
it. I thought often of Highbury's nighttime lovers (I was the day shift)
and how the pleasure of our experiences and longings might intertwine.'

Berry's advice to poets starting out is to 'be tough on your poems
but kind to yourself… Listen to poems being spoken, let their electricity
light you'. Berry's unforgettable final image of the lover taken by the
wind – 'stripped and blown, / then jilted dazzling in the arms of the
trees' – is surely a prime example of that illuminating electricity.

Mary Jean Chan (b. 1990 Hong Kong) is a Ledbury Poetry Critic,
editor of *Oxford Poetry*, and a lecturer in creative writing at Oxford
Brookes University. The 'window' of her poem's title represents, among
other things, a threshold: the speaker 'struggles with facets of their
identity (i.e. queerness) but chooses to survive, and the window crystallises
precisely what it is that the living do – that they choose love, reconciliation,
and the stubborn – often painfully complex – realities of living'.

In 2017, Chan was shortlisted for the Forward Prize for Best Single
Poem, becoming the youngest shortlistee in the prize's history. Her first
collection, *Flèche*, is forthcoming from Faber (2019).

Jonathan Edwards (b. 1979 Newport) is an English teacher. His poem
'Bridge' is a monologue in the voice of one of the bridges from his
hometown of Newport: 'I bear the city's weight here on my back, / all
these commuting cars and belching vans.' A touching attentiveness to
small absurdist details ('the acupuncture of a gentle moped') does not
obscure a deeper seriousness: of a potential suicide, the bridge reports,
'I know by heart, exactly / what it is to just have too much weight to bear.'

Edwards won the Costa Prize for Poetry in 2015 for his debut
collection, *My Family and Other Superheroes*, and his second collection,
Gen, was nominated for Wales Book of the Year.

Parwana Fayyaz (b. 1990 Kabul, Afghanistan) was raised in Pakistan, and is currently working towards a PhD on the medieval Persian poet Jami at Trinity College, Cambridge. 'Forty Names', her shortlisted poem, draws inspiration both narrative and lyrical from those medieval Persian traditions; Fayyaz heard the story from her parents when she was a child. 'It is about a mountain called *kohi chehal dokhtaran*, the forty girls' mountain. My poem tries to re-narrate the story by giving the forty women their names, a lamp and their colourful scarves.'

Fayyaz graduated with a BA and an MA in comparative literature, creative writing and religious studies from Stanford University, studying under Eavan Boland. She intends to stay in academia to pursue her studies of Persian Sufi poetry, and work towards her first collection.

Holly Pester (b. 1982 Colchester) works as a practice-based researcher; she's completed residences in the Text Art Archive, the Women's Art Library and the Wellcome Collection. 'Comic Timing', her shortlisted poem, takes for its subject an early medical abortion, a 'banal and farcical one'. '[A]che is tempo / I have seen millions of films / I get it,' she writes, as the rhythms of her retelling translate into the rhythms of the 'bodily-yet-politicised experience'.

The poets Pester most admires, in her own words, practise 'formal experimentation in time with lived experience, which becomes a new thought and an expression of a politics, and sometimes, also, a form of comedy (as an affect on life)'. She is currently working on a new collection, from which 'Comic Timing' is taken, 'all around latency and radical rest states'.

Publisher acknowledgements

Gary Allen · Technically Speaking · *The Glass King* · Stairwell Books

Rachael Allen · Many Bird Roast · *Kingdomland* · Faber & Faber

Raymond Antrobus · The Perseverance · Happy Birthday Moon ·
   The Perseverance · Penned in the Margins

Fatimah Asghar · Partition · *If They Come for Us* ·
   Corsair, Little, Brown Book Group

Zohar Atkins · Letting Nothing Wait · *Nineveh* · Carcanet

Fiona Benson · [personal: speedo] · Eurofighter Typhoon ·
   Vertigo & Ghost · Cape Poetry

Jay Bernard · Pace · Sentence · *Surge* · Chatto & Windus

Liz Berry · Highbury Park · Wild Court

Zoë Brigley · Blind Horse Elegy · *HAND & SKULL* · Bloodaxe Books

Jericho Brown · Monotheism · *The Tradition* · Picador Poetry

David Cain · 4.06pm · 4.15pm · *Truth Street* · Smokestack Books

Niall Campbell · Clapping Game · The Night Watch · *Noctuary* ·
   Bloodaxe Books

Mary Jean Chan · The Window · The National Poetry Competition/
   The Poetry Society

Nick Drake · Through the Red Light · *Out of Range* · Bloodaxe Books

Carol Ann Duffy · Empty Nest · *Sincerity* · Picador Poetry

Jonathan Edwards · Bridge · *The Frogmore Papers*

Inua Ellams · extract from *The Half-God of Rainfall* ·
   HarperCollins /4th Estate

Martina Evans · Love · *Poetry Ireland Review*

Shangyang Fang · Argument of Situations · Gregory O'Donoghue
   Competition

Parwana Fayyaz · Forty Names · *PN Review*

fukudapero · untitled · *flowers like blue glass* · Crocus Books

Isabel Galleymore · The Starfish · Significant Other · *Significant Other* ·
   Carcanet

Peter Gizzi · The Present Is Constant Elegy · *The Poetry Review*

Rebecca Goss · Rachel · *Girl* · Carcanet

Lavinia Greenlaw · The break · *The Built Moment* · Faber & Faber

Vona Groarke · No one uses doilies anymore · *DOUBLE NEGATIVE* ·
   The Gallery Press

Scott Manley Hadley · untitled · *BAD BOY POET* · Open Pen
Matthew Haigh · Do You Even Lift Bro? · *Death Magazine* ·
    Salt Publishing
Robert Hamberger · Unpacking the books · *Blue Wallpaper* ·
    Waterloo Press
Nafeesa Hamid · Doctor's appointment · *Besharam* · Verve Poetry Press
Rob Hindle · The Tapestry Makers of Flanders · *The Grail Roads* ·
    Longbarrow Press
Sarah Hymas · Whale-boned Corset and Other Relics ·
    And Other Poems
Chloë Alys Irwin · Hellingly Asylum, 1952 · *Neon Literary Magazine*
Maria Jastrzębska · The Subsongs of Crow · *Poetry Wales*
Ilya Kaminsky · We Lived Happily during the War · Deafness,
    an Insurgency, Begins · *Deaf Republic* · Faber & Faber
Luke Kennard · Crow Baby · *The Scores*
John Kinsella · Milking the Tiger Snake · *Insomnia* · Picador Poetry
Neetha Kunaratnam · The Afterlife · *Just Because* · Smokestack Books
Fiona Larkin · Rope of Sand · South Bank Poetry
Thyrza Leyshon · Edith Sitwell · Ware Poets Competition
    (Rockingham Press)
Ada Limón · A Name · *The Carrying* · Corsair, Little, Brown
    Book Group
Theresa Lola · wikiHow To Mourn: Mourning in Healthy Ways ·
    In Search of Equilibrium · Nine Arches Press
Thomas McCarthy · Thigh-Bone of a Deer · *Prophecy* · Carcanet
Kei Miller · To Know Green From Green · *In Nearby Bushes* · Carcanet
Ciarán O'Rourke · The Cure For Nettles · *The Buried Breath* ·
    The Irish Pages Press
Morgan Parker · I Feel Most Colored When I Am Thrown Against
    a Sharp White Background · *MAGICAL NEGRO* · Corsair, Little,
    Brown Book Group
Sandeep Parmar · An Uncommon Language · *The Poetry Review*
Holly Pester · Comic Timing · *Granta*
DA Prince · The Window · *SOUTH Poetry Magazine*
Vidyan Ravinthiran · Today · Aubade · *The Million-petalled Flower
    of Being Here* · Bloodaxe Books
Deryn Rees-Jones · Firebird · *Erato* · Seren

Sophie Robinson · FUCKING UP ON THE ROCKS · *RABBIT* ·
  Boiler House Press · excerpt from Larry Rivers' eulogy to
  Frank O'Hara as transcribed by the *New York Times*
Stephen Sexton · Cheese Bridge Area · Front Door · *If All the World and
  Love Were Young* · Penguin Books
Maria Sledmere · Ariosos for Lavish Matter · *Blackbox Manifold*
Austin Smith · American Glue Factory · *Flyover Country* ·
  Princeton University Press
Jean Sprackland · April · *Green Noise* · Jonathan Cape
Julian Stannard · Eau Sauvage · *Ambit*
Rebecca Tamás · WITCH FIRE · *WITCH* · Penned in the Margins
Adam Thorpe · Chinooks · *Words from the Wall* · Jonathan Cape
Helen Tookey · City of Departures · Letter to Anna · *City of Departures* ·
  Carcanet
RA Villanueva · Namesake · *The Rialto*
Rebecca Watts · Red Gloves · *Times Literary Supplement*
Hugo Williams · Shadow Pack · *Lines Off* · Faber & Faber
Alison Winch · Bishop Berkeley is My Boyfriend · *Darling, It's Me* ·
  Penned in the Margins
Ann Wroe · At San Damiano · *FRANCIS: A Life in Songs* · Jonathan Cape

Winners of the Forward Prizes

Best Collection

2018 · Danez Smith · *Don't Call Us Dead* · Chatto & Windus
2017 · Sinéad Morrissey · *On Balance* · Carcanet
2016 · Vahni Capildeo · *Measures of Expatriation* · Carcanet
2015 · Claudia Rankine · *Citizen: An American Lyric* · Penguin Books
2014 · Kei Miller · *The Cartographer Tries to Map a Way to Zion* · Carcanet
2013 · Michael Symmons Roberts · *Drysalter* · Cape Poetry
2012 · Jorie Graham · *PLACE* · Carcanet
2011 · John Burnside · *Black Cat Bone* · Cape Poetry
2010 · Seamus Heaney · *Human Chain* · Faber & Faber
2009 · Don Paterson · *Rain* · Faber & Faber
2008 · Mick Imlah · *The Lost Leader* · Faber & Faber
2007 · Sean O'Brien · *The Drowned Book* · Picador Poetry
2006 · Robin Robertson · *Swithering* · Picador Poetry
2005 · David Harsent · *Legion* · Faber & Faber
2004 · Kathleen Jamie · *The Tree House* · Picador Poetry
2003 · Ciaran Carson · *Breaking News* · The Gallery Press
2002 · Peter Porter · *Max is Missing* · Picador Poetry
2001 · Sean O'Brien · *Downriver* · Picador Poetry
2000 · Michael Donaghy · *Conjure* · Picador Poetry
1999 · Jo Shapcott · *My Life Asleep* · OUP
1998 · Ted Hughes · *Birthday Letters* · Faber & Faber
1997 · Jamie McKendrick · *The Marble Fly* · OUP
1996 · John Fuller · *Stones and Fires* · Chatto & Windus
1995 · Sean O'Brien · *Ghost Train* · OUP
1994 · Alan Jenkins · *Harm* · Chatto & Windus
1993 · Carol Ann Duffy · *Mean Time* · Anvil Press
1992 · Thom Gunn · *The Man with Night Sweats* · Faber & Faber

Best First Collection

2018 · Phoebe Power · *Shrines of Upper Austria* · Carcanet

2017 · Ocean Vuong · *Night Sky with Exit Wounds* · Cape Poetry

2016 · Tiphanie Yanique · *Wife* · Peepal Tree

2015 · Mona Arshi · *Small Hands* · Pavilion Poetry

2014 · Liz Berry · *Black Country* · Chatto & Windus

2013 · Emily Berry · *Dear Boy* · Faber & Faber

2012 · Sam Riviere · *81 Austerities* · Faber & Faber

2011 · Rachael Boast · *Sidereal* · Picador Poetry

2010 · Hilary Menos · *Berg* · Seren

2009 · Emma Jones · *The Striped World* · Faber & Faber

2008 · Kathryn Simmonds · *Sunday at the Skin Launderette* · Seren

2007 · Daljit Nagra · *Look We Have Coming to Dover!* · Faber & Faber

2006 · Tishani Doshi · *Countries of the Body* · Aark Arts

2005 · Helen Farish · *Intimates* · Cape Poetry

2004 · Leontia Flynn · *These Days* · Cape Poetry

2003 · AB Jackson · *Fire Stations* · Anvil Press

2002 · Tom French · *Touching the Bones* · The Gallery Press

2001 · John Stammers · *Panoramic Lounge-Bar* · Picador Poetry

2000 · Andrew Waterhouse · *In* · The Rialto

1999 · Nick Drake · *The Man in the White Suit* · Bloodaxe Books

1998 · Paul Farley · *The Boy from the Chemist is Here to See You* · Picador Poetry

1997 · Robin Robertson · *A Painted Field* · Picador Poetry

1996 · Kate Clanchy · *Slattern* · Chatto & Windus

1995 · Jane Duran · *Breathe Now, Breathe* · Enitharmon

1994 · Kwame Dawes · *Progeny of Air* · Peepal Tree

1993 · Don Paterson · *Nil Nil* · Faber & Faber

1992 · Simon Armitage · *Kid* · Faber & Faber

Best Single Poem

2018 · Liz Berry · The Republic of Motherhood · *Granta*

2017 · Ian Patterson · The Plenty of Nothing · *PN Review*

2016 · Sasha Dugdale · Joy · *PN Review*

2015 · Claire Harman · The Mighty Hudson · *Times Literary Supplement*

2014 · Stephen Santus · In a Restaurant · Bridport Prize

2013 · Nick MacKinnon · The Metric System · *The Warwick Review*

2012 · Denise Riley · A Part Song · *London Review of Books*

2011 · RF Langley · To a Nightingale · *London Review of Books*

2010 · Julia Copus · An Easy Passage · *Magma*

2009 · Robin Robertson · At Roane Head · *London Review of Books*

2008 · Don Paterson · Love Poem for Natalie "Tusja" Beridze · *The Poetry Review*

2007 · Alice Oswald · Dunt · *Poetry London*

2006 · Sean O'Brien · Fantasia on a Theme of James Wright · *The Poetry Review*

2005 · Paul Farley · Liverpool Disappears for a Billionth of a Second · *The North*

2004 · Daljit Nagra · Look We Have Coming to Dover! · *The Poetry Review*

2003 · Robert Minhinnick · The Fox in the Museum of Wales · *Poetry London*

2002 · Medbh McGuckian · She Is in the Past, She Has This Grace · *The Shop*

2001 · Ian Duhig · The Lammas Hireling · National Poetry Competition

2000 · Tessa Biddington · The Death of Descartes · Bridport Prize

1999 · Robert Minhinnick · Twenty-five Laments for Iraq · *PN Review*

1998 · Sheenagh Pugh · Envying Owen Beattie · *New Welsh Review*

1997 · Lavinia Greenlaw · A World Where News Travelled Slowly · *Times Literary Supplement*

1996 · Kathleen Jamie · The Graduates · *Times Literary Supplement*

1995 · Jenny Joseph · In Honour of Love · *The Rialto*

1994 · Iain Crichton Smith · Autumn · *PN Review*

1993 · Vicki Feaver · Judith · *Independent on Sunday*

1992 · Jackie Kay · Black Bottom · Bloodaxe Books

Supporting Poetry Through This Book

Proceeds from the sale of this book go towards the Forward Arts Foundation, which promotes public knowledge, understanding and enjoyment of poetry in the UK and Ireland. We are a charity committed to widening poetry's audience, honouring achievement and supporting talent: our programmes include National Poetry Day and the Forward Prizes for Poetry. Through our projects we work with schools, libraries, publishers and members of the public across the British Isles.

For more detail and further reading about the Forward Prizes, books and associated programmes, see our website forwardartsfoundation.org or follow us on Facebook or Twitter @ForwardPrizes